50
YEARS
OF HUME
SCHOLARSHIP

FIFTY
YEARS OF
HUME
SCHOLARSHIP

A Bibliographical Guide
by ROLAND HALL

EDINBURGH

University
Press

•

© Roland Hall 1978
Edinburgh University Press
22 George Square, Edinburgh

ISBN 0 85224 337 5

Printed in Great Britain
by W. & J. Mackay Limited
Chatham

CONTENTS

•

*A man will turn over half a library
to make one book*

Johnson

•

PREFACE

MY BIBLIOGRAPHICAL WORK on the Hume literature began
as an experiment, but continued in response to demand. The
present book is partly based on my earlier publication, *A Hume
Bibliography, from 1930* (York, 1971). (This is still available,
direct from the author.)

A later collection of material, which was eventually published
as 'More Hume Bibliography' in the *Philosophical Quarterly* for
January 1976 (Hume Bicentenary Issue), has also been incorpor-
ated in the present book, repairing many omissions in the original
bibliography and also extending it up to 1975. Further, a considerable list of works that were published during 1976 (the
bicentenary year) has now been added, although what is known
to me at present from so recent a year may well turn out to be in-
complete. The present new version of the bibliography has been
enlarged by five years at the beginning too, so that it runs from
1925 (fifty-two years in all).

In addition to dealing with the Hume literature from 1925 to
1976, I have also provided a list of the main writings on Hume
for the period 1900–1924; unlike the main bibliography, this
does not aim at completeness, and lacks some small details. It
does, however, contain several newly-found items.

I should of course make it clear that, besides the extensions
and additions to the main bibliography that I have mentioned,
the present listing has a great many entirely new entries, as well
as further additions, corrections, and improvements throughout.
These are mainly the result of a very thorough revision—lasting
more than a year—of the earlier treatment of the material.

Systematic revision has also doubled the length of the subject
index. This index, it is important to stress, does not refer merely
to the wording of the titles in the bibliography, but is as far as
possible an index to the contents of the books and articles them-
selves. This is the most unusual, and ambitious, feature of the
present book. The occasional humour of the subject index
should not be taken as a sign of general frivolity. In fact, making
it constantly required a difficult exercise of judgement, and the

result may not be to everyone's satisfaction; but I hope that some readers will be uniquely assisted by it. Altogether, the entries in the bibliography are indexed three ways: by author, language and subject. The author index and the language index were not present in the 1971 book, and were added at the revision stage. The indexes have subsequently been extended to cover the 1900–24 list. The provision of an author index might seem superfluous, but does of course, apart from the more obvious uses, have the advantage that if any item has been assigned to the wrong date, or to a date not expected by the reader (where this is arbitrary), its entry can still be found easily by using this index; which may help to obviate the mistaken impression that such items are missing.

Additional guidance to the Hume literature is now provided by the introductory essay on the development of Hume scholarship. This indicates, among other matters, which are the main books on Hume of this and earlier periods; points out some vexed questions, and where they have been discussed; and also identifies the best modern editions of the main works of Hume.

Several friends and correspondents, from various countries, contributed information towards the previous publications, as described in the prefaces of 1971 and 1976, and I would like to thank them again for their help. I have also obtained several entries and review references from the commendable work of Dr E. Ronchetti (1967). For the present reworking, which had to be carried on for the most part alongside teaching duties and other commitments such as the editing of the *Locke Newsletter*, I was mainly dependent on the use of the university library (including its interloan service) and my own books. Even at this stage, however, I was not without help from others: those who supplied material, and in some cases offered criticisms and suggestions, were Ronald Atkinson, John W. Davis, Neil Dumbleton, Pat Henderson, Peter Jones, Peter Nidditch, Sandy Stewart, and my daughter Rosalind, and I am very grateful to them. I wish particularly to thank my colleague Anthony Price, who was kind enough to check a number of early items in the Bodleian Library. I am also very grateful to Jennifer Denton for typing the introductory essay and the indexes. And I wish to thank my colleagues Andrew Ward and Roger Woolhouse, as well as Anthony Price, for their criticisms of the introductory essay.

In spite of the extreme care taken in revising the bibliographical catalogue, there will inevitably be some undetected errors in it. Apart from errors introduced by human weakness in reading and transcription, this is chiefly because I was not able to obtain or inspect all the items listed, and often had to depend instead on the information given by reference works. (These were obviously not wholly reliable, since they frequently conflicted.) I have, however, personally examined the majority of the items entered in the main list. (There are some fifteen hundred entries in it altogether.)

The aim of the work is in no sense antiquarian; it is intended to be an aid to the study of Hume. In consequence, bibliographical details are in general kept to the minimum necessary for locating the material, except that the length of books is often indicated by giving the number of pages.

No other bibliography covers the same period of the secondary literature on Hume. What is more, no one else at all has previously reported on the Hume publications of the decade 1967–76. As for the years that had already been covered by previous workers in this field, it should be pointed out that quite a large proportion of the material for those years in the present work is not to be found in any of those collections. Moreover, there is a vital difference in the presentation: even the material that others had collected previously, when presented as it is here, with cross-references, review information, and indexes, is made really accessible for the first time.

ACKNOWLEDGEMENTS

In the final months before going to press, I made requests to several foreign libraries and individual scholars for information. Those who were kind enough to meet my requests were Dr F. Hiorth, Professor G.H.von Wright, the Central University Library, Bucharest, Professor G.Nuchelmans, the Jagellonian Library of Cracow, the Semmelweis Museum, Budapest, Dr J. Bjarup, Professor S.Castignone, Professor A.Pavković, Professor H.Regnéll, Professor S.Rábade Romeo, and Dr J.de Salas Ortueta. For help in proof-reading, I wish to thank my wife, Daphne, and my colleagues Ronald Atkinson, Roger Woolhouse, and Susan Mendus.

R.H. *University of York*

ABBREVIATIONS

Two systems of abbreviation for journal titles are used in the bibliography. In the main part of an entry, short-ened titles, based on British Standard recommenda-tions, are used; these are intended to be self-explanatory. In the subsidiary part of the entry, where references are listed within square brackets, most titles have been re-duced to initials, for economy of space. These initials are listed below, alongside the full titles.

AGP. Archiv für Geschichte der Philosophie
AJP. Australasian Journal of Philosophy
APQ. American Philosophical Quarterly
ASM. Anales del Seminario de Metafísica
CC. Civiltà Cattolica
D. Dialogue
E. Ethics
ELH. English Literary History
GCFI. Giornale Critico della Filosofia Italiana
HJ. Hibbert Journal
JHI. Journal of the History of Ideas
JHP. Journal of the History of Philosophy
JP. Journal of Philosophy
JVI. Journal of Value Inquiry
KS. Kant-Studien
M. Mind
MLN. Modern Language Notes
MLR. Modern Language Review
MS. Modern Schoolman
NQ. Notes and Queries
NS. New Scholasticism
P. Philosophy

PAS. Proceedings of the Aristotelian Society
PB. Philosophical Books
PMLA. Proceedings of the Modern Language Association
PPR. Philosophy and Phenomeno-logical Research
PQ. Philosophical Quarterly
PR. Philosophical Review
PS. Political Studies
PSt. Philosophical Studies
RCSF. Rivista Critica di Scienze Filosofiche
RES. Review of English Studies
RFNS. Rivista di Filosofia neo-scolastica
RIP. Revue Internationale de Philosophie
RLC. Revue de littérature comparée
RM. Review of Metaphysics
RMM. Revue de Métaphysique et de Morale
RP. Revue Philosophique (de la France et de l'Étranger)
RPL. Revue Philosophique de Louvain
RS. Religious Studies
T. Theoria
TLS. Times Literary Supplement

THE DEVELOPMENT OF
HUME SCHOLARSHIP

IT WAS ONLY in the second quarter of the present century that Hume came into his own as a great philosopher, worthy of regular discussion. Before 1925, books about him in his own language were relatively few. After waking Kant from his dogmatic slumbers, Hume's own philosophical work passed through the nineteenth century in suspended animation. Whether Mill read the *Treatise* has been doubted;[1] and also whether Huxley understood it. Admittedly, Green and Grose edited the philosophical works, but they nullified the effect by introducing them with a book-length attempt at refutation.[2] Although more than a hundred books and articles on Hume appeared before 1925, the great majority of these were not in English;[3] indeed, many were the product of the German thesis-industry, the main places of publication being Halle, Leipzig and Berlin.

Even after 1900, work on Hume was predominantly Continental or American.[4] The outstanding, almost solitary, exception was Kemp Smith, who came forward in *Mind* (1905) as the champion of 'natural belief', unjustifiable by reason, as being 'perhaps the most characteristic doctrine' in Hume.[5] Although Hume also attracted an occasional paper from Moore, Broad and Whitehead, no one could say that these discussions were closely related to the texts.[6] Later, as a professor at Princeton, Kemp Smith encouraged C. W. Hendel to work on Hume: at first on a doctoral dissertation, afterwards on the fairly extensive *Studies* (1925).

Hendel's *Studies* was the first of many general books in English on Hume's philosophy, some of which were scholarly contributions (Laing 1932; Laird 1932; Kemp Smith 1941; Passmore 1952; Capaldi 1975; Penelhum 1975), while others were mainly introductory (Macnabb 1951; Basson 1958; Price 1968). General books on Hume have also been written in many other languages, notably German (Metz 1929), Italian (Dal Pra 1949; Santucci 1969), French (Leroy 1953; Malherbe 1976), Dutch (Snethlage 1963; Nuchelmans 1965), Swedish (Brunius 1956) and Norwegian (Hiorth 1973).[7] Of all the general books mentioned,

Kemp Smith's *The Philosophy of David Hume* (1941), proposing as it does a definite view of Hume's doctrines, and being firmly based on the texts, still towers above all the rest, and is essential to any serious study of Hume. Among the others, the most useful is probably Laird's *Hume's Philosophy of Human Nature* (1932), for its detailed discussion and historical information. The books by Capaldi and Penelhum, however, provide fresh and interesting readings of Hume in the central areas of his philosophy, while Leroy is a valuable work that discusses all parts of Hume's thought.

Books on a limited field may be more likely to advance understanding of the part of Hume's philosophy they deal with. Some books have dealt with a part of Hume's epistemology (that is, perception, knowledge, belief) alone (Maund 1937; Price 1940). Others have been primarily concerned with his metaphysics— in the sense of his doctrines of existence, substance, causality, and so on—(Church 1935; Anderson 1966). One book, because it is a study of the first *Inquiry*, discusses much of both subjects, and can therefore be regarded as an account of Hume's theoretical philosophy (the term used in my Subject Index for this main division of philosophy).[8] The book in question (Flew 1961) is undoubtedly the best of the limited studies, standing out for its liveliness, clarity, and incisive philosophical argument. In addition, Price (1940) is a valuable and ingenious philosophical exercise; it deserves not to be neglected. Other studies have been concerned with Hume's ethics, either as a whole (Glathe 1950) or in some part or aspect (Kydd 1946; Broiles 1964; Árdal 1966; Mercer 1972; Tweyman 1974; Harrison 1976).[9] Árdal has been the most widely acclaimed of these. An important book on Hume's Newtonian background and his method, and the later changes in his thinking, is Noxon (1973). On the specific subject of Hume's argument for scepticism about induction, Stove's monograph (1973) is indispensable.

The other main areas of Hume's thought have not been very well supplied with specialised books. (a) His activity as a historian is discussed, and illustrated with excerpts from all parts of his writings, in Norton & Popkin (1965); and the *History* receives some extended discussion in Forbes (1975), which is primarily concerned with Hume's politics in relation to natural law. (But one might have expected to find by now a book on Hume's performance as a historian, by a historian.) (b) An earlier book (Stewart 1963) treats of the whole of Hume's political theory, bringing in the economics to some extent. In Italian there is Giarrizzo (1962) on Hume's politics and history;

in French there is Vlachos (1955) on the politics. But there is no book-length account of Hume's political theory that is really suited to the needs of philosophers. (c) As for religion, much the same can be said: parts of books (for example of Flew 1961) are devoted to Hume's thought on this subject, but apart from an account that mostly relates that to its background in the theology of the time (Hurlbutt 1965) there is no proper study in English; although in French and Italian there are Leroy (1929) and Carabelli (1972). This deficiency, however, is soon to be remedied: a book by Gaskin on Hume's philosophy of religion is about to be published. (d) On Hume's aesthetics, there are the small Brunius (1952) in English and the vast Brunet (1965) in French, neither of which has received much praise; while from a literary point of view J.V.Price has interestingly examined the use of the ironic mode in Hume's writings generally (1965). On all these parts of Hume's thought—history, politics, religion, aesthetics—the more interesting discussions have on the whole been those published in journals.

Indeed, on all aspects of Hume the journal (and collection) article has become increasingly important. The controversies that still persist over Hume's main positions are typically found in the journals, and the quantity of discussion there is much greater than, for instance, the amount devoted to Locke.[10] The most striking feature of Hume scholarship is the extent of disagreement. Hume is clearly an exceedingly difficult philosopher to interpret, as Selby-Bigge pointed out in 1894, when he concluded that it is 'easy to find all philosophies in Hume, or . . . none at all'.[11]

Certain authors, however, have made progress in elucidating a topic; they offer in their articles a close and thorough examination of parts of Hume's text, and take us markedly beyond our previous understanding of it: for example, Cook on Hume's scepticism with regard to the senses (1968), Popkin on his Pyrrhonism (1951), Flew on Hume on miracles (1959), Butler on natural belief (1960), and Pike on evil (1963). Some more recent articles that probably deserve special praise on similar grounds are Norton on Hume's common sense morality (1975), Jones on his aesthetics (1976), Davidson on his theory of pride (1976), and Gaskin on his critique of religion (1976).

Besides these *tours de force*, there have been various running debates or repeated scrutinies that have helped to clarify certain puzzling topics in Hume, for example his views on mathematics (Atkinson 1960; Zabeeh 1950 & 1964; Flew 1966), on causality (for references to the very extensive discussion of this topic, see the Subject Index), and on personal identity (Penelhum 1955; Pike 1967; Noxon 1970; Brett 1972; Ashley & Stack 1974; Wolfram 1974; Pears 1975; Penelhum 1975 & 1976; to name but some). Two other important questions on which progress has been made through a series of journal contributions—and which in spite of their historical nature are bound to affect the understanding of Hume's philosophy—are, what the relation is between the *Treatise* and the *Inquiries* (Kemp Smith 1939; Nelson 1972; Cummins 1973; King 1976), and whether Hume read Berkeley and made some use of him (Wiener, Popkin, Mossner 1959; Flew, Wiener, Bracken 1961; Popkin 1964; Hall 1967 & 1968; Conroy 1969; Hall 1970; Morrisroe 1973).[12]

Again, the controversy as to what Hume meant in the famous passage about *Is* and *Ought* (*Treatise* III.i.1, ad fin.) has developed, after the casual references and rather bold assertions of the early fifties, into careful attempts to interpret the passage in the light of its context and of Hume's ethical views generally. It has recently even been maintained that the *Is*-and-*Ought* debaters were, most of them, missing the point, since Hume rejected the moral 'ought' in the sense required (Capaldi 1966 & 1975; Moonan 1975).

Another question that has been discussed incessantly—one might have hoped it would be finally settled by now—is which speaker represents Hume in the *Dialogues concerning Natural Religion*. Is it Cleanthes or Philo? Early commentators usually plumped for one or the other (for example Dugald Stewart, Burton, Laing, for Cleanthes; Leslie Stephen, Kemp Smith, and later Flew, for Philo) and did so with surprising assurance.[13] The difficulties have driven some to favour a combination of the two characters; while a recent view is that Hume is so deeply agnostic that none of the characters speaks for him, but that on the contrary he himself regards the dispute between Philo and Cleanthes as futile and the questions raised as unanswerable (Noxon 1964).[14] At the other extreme, there are those who are tempted to regard Hume as in some way religious (Jessop 1974), a piece of wishful thinking anticipated by Lechartier in 1900 and first thought of by Boswell, in a dream.[15] The divergence of opinion among those who have worked closely and for many years on the *Dialogues* reflects the continuing uncertainty about Hume's overall philosophical position and intentions, above all in matters of religion and epistemology.[16] Perhaps this uncertainty is irremovable; but if it could be removed, that would only be by applying new methods of investigative scholarship.[17]

Whatever Hume's intentions may have been, it is clear that

his work is now being treated seriously. With luck, we are now out of the period when solemn glorification contrasted with vitriolic attack.[18] A general attempt to consolidate the results already obtained would now be appropriate, and it is one of the aims of the present book to make that possible.

Apart from discussion of his views, there are many other ways of contributing to Hume scholarship. The most important is the editing of his writings. The best modern editions of the main works are now to be identified, a task that takes up the rest of this paragraph. (1) The best edition of the *Treatise* is that by Selby-Bigge, produced before the period under review. Close scrutiny has shown the text to be almost wholly reliable, unlike the other modern editions of this work.[19] Among its pleasing features are the side-headings, which facilitate reference, and the extremely valuable analytical index.[20] (2) The Selby-Bigge edition of the *Enquiries*, on the other hand, was not so reliable. But it has recently appeared with a revised text (Nidditch 1975). This revised Selby-Bigge is now the most accurate edition of the *Enquiries*, and the first with regular annotations. It too has an analytical index. It also has comparative tables of contents, for the *Enquiries* and the *Treatise*. Hume's additions and subtractions to the original editions are recorded in Hendel's editions of the two *Enquiries* (1955, 1957), although the texts in these contain many errors. (3) The Kemp Smith edition of the *Dialogues* (Kemp Smith 1935), was the first to make use of the MS, and is probably still the best; it provides a discussion and analysis as long as the text itself. The new edition from the MS (Price 1976) has been fiercely criticised for unreliability.[21] (4) Hume's *Essays, Moral, Political, and Literary* have not been properly edited, and the best text may still be that in the Green and Grose *Philosophical Works*. There is a convenient pocket edition (1903, in the 'World's Classics' series; reprinted 1963, Oxford). There are also collections of the political essays (Hendel 1953) and the literary and other essays (Lenz 1965), with introductions; unfortunately, the texts in these are mainly based on the collected philosophical works of 1826. Thirteen of the political essays also appear, modernised and shorn of footnotes, but allegedly reprinted from the 1777 edition, in Watkins (1951). (5) The *History of England* lacks a modern edition. However, the first volume published has been handily reprinted (Forbes 1970) from the first edition (1754), when it was entitled '*The History of Great Britain*, Vol. I'.[22] It contains the reigns of James I and Charles I; most of the volumes written later by Hume describe earlier reigns, so it constitutes one of the final sections of the eventual work. Some excerpts from the complete *History* are to be found in Norton & Popkin (1965); there is also an abridgement of the *History* by Kilcup (1975). (6) Of the *Natural History of Religion*, Colver (1976) must now be the best edition, even though it is not completely accurate.

In the fifty years under review, more of Hume's own writing has become known. Assiduous collection has resulted in *The Letters of David Hume* in two volumes (Greig 1932) and the *New Letters* (Klibansky & Mossner 1954). Publication of letters still continues (notably, Mossner 1958; Kozanecki 1963; Morrisroe 1973; Price 1974; for the rest see the Subject Index, s.v. Letters). More remarkably, two printed but anonymous works of Hume have at last come to light again during this period, two centuries after their original publication and disappearance: the *Abstract* (1740) of the *Treatise*, republished by Keynes & Sraffa (1938), and *A Letter from a Gentleman to his Friend in Edinburgh* (1745), republished by Mossner and Price (1967).[23] As well as these additions to the body of his work, we now have more exact knowledge of his intentions in certain minor respects: Hume's own corrections to the *Treatise*—apart from those printed in Volume Three of the first edition—are now available (fully reported in Nidditch 1976). Some were found in a copy in California (Nethery 1963); but most remarkably, a duplicate copy of Volume Three of the *Treatise*, that came to light in the British Museum in 1971 because of a binding error, contained over a hundred corrections in Hume's own hand (Connon 1975). And from the same volume some corrections to the *Abstract*—which was bound in with the *Treatise*—first became known. These corrections also were in Hume's own hand (Connon 1976).

Other important contributions to the study of Hume made in recent decades have been the Mossner *Life* (1954), and the founding of a special journal, *Hume Studies* (1975–).[24] Lastly, the increasing flood of material during the fifty years has necessitated the bibliographical work that began with Metz (1926, 1928) and Jessop (1938) and has continued chiefly with Ronchetti (1967) and the present writer (1971, 1976, and this book).

What special needs remain? A major desideratum is a full-scale study in English of Hume on religion. (However, as was said earlier, one is due to appear shortly.) There is room, too, for a really illuminating book on Hume's aesthetics. Another desideratum, in my opinion, is a biography of a different type from Mossner's. His book, since it contains so much information, will of course remain a vital work of reference, and must form the basis of any future attempt; but one hopes that as our understanding of Hume's thought and character improves, the massive bulk of Mossner (1954) will not deter another—possibly a regular author of biographies, possibly someone with a philosophical axe to grind—from going over the ground again,[25] and writing a less cluttered, more explanatory life.

In the long run, of course, we ought to have a Collected Works and a Concordance;[26] but the immediate need is for a philosophical commentary on the *Treatise*. To be of use, this would need to inform the reader of the *Treatise* continually about its language, its sources, the structure of the argument, parallel passages, and the interpretations that have been offered; as is done for Aristotle or Kant.

One might suppose that with all the progress I have described in detailed exegesis, editions, and aids to scholarship, Hume would have become one of the most influential philosophers of this century. This has not been the case, although of course he has received very widespread attention, as is shown by the work listed in this book. The philosopher whose native language is English may, indeed, wonder at the inclusion of entries for works in nineteen other languages, these being mostly unnecessary for his immediate purposes; but such inclusiveness is *de rigueur*, now that the study of Hume is world-wide.

In Britain, however, it is remarkable that, far from being a great influence during this century, Hume has merely commanded general respect among philosophers, often as a supposed forerunner of logical positivism. He has had virtually no influence at all on the most prominent philosophers of the time, with the exception of Ayer and Price. Russell was not really concerned with him;[27] Wittgenstein and Austin rejected him as useless for their purposes.[28] Ryle does sometimes refer to him in *The Concept of Mind*, and once wrote an appreciation of him (Ryle 1956), but never engages in print in any close study. What is the explanation of the lack of honour, or, at any rate, serious attention, from these men, the leading thinkers of his own country, or rather, of 'this island' (Hume's own expression)? They did no work on him, partly because of an arguably healthy tendency to disregard the actual historical detail of the classic philosophers, in favour of making original contributions, and partly because they selected other candidates for scholarly treatment or private study: in particular, they preferred to work on Plato, Leibniz, Kant and Frege. There is a vicious circle in this: in Oxford Hume has sometimes been thought second-rate, but this may result from his being insufficiently studied there.

However, a considerable amount of serious work on Hume is

going on in many universities, mostly in Britain and North America. As published work on this great philosopher becomes increasingly precise, accurate and philosophically rewarding, he may for the first time since the eighteenth century[29] have an important influence on the development of philosophy.

Notes and References

1. 'There is no cause for surprise when we find that John Stuart Mill had never been sufficiently interested in Hume to look into the *Treatise* for himself, and seemingly had also never read Hume's *Dialogues*' (Kemp Smith 1941, p. 521); 'Mill knew practically nothing of Hume' (J. Passmore, *A Hundred Years of Philosophy*, 1957, p. 11); 'John Stuart Mill apparently never thought to open it [the *Treatise*]' (Mossner 1969, p. 26).

   These remarks perhaps derive ultimately from Leslie Stephen's judgement of a footnote by Mill. 'A note to the concluding chapter of the *Examination of Hamilton*', says Stephen, 'seems to imply that he [Mill] was not acquainted with the *Treatise*; nor does he appear from his posthumous essays to have studied Hume's writings upon theology' (*The English Utilitarians*, [1900], vol. III, p. 86 fn.).

   It is of course probable that Kant too, though he read the *Enquiries* and other works, failed to look at the *Treatise*; he was awakened by quotations from it in a translation of Beattie's work.

2. Now available actually as a separate book: Thomas Hill Green, *Hume and Locke* (New York 1968). This consists of a photographic reprint (without the sidenotes, but these merely repeat the Contents) of Green's two introductions to the main divisions of the *Treatise*, from vols. 1–2 of the *Philosophical Works* (1874; photographic reprint 1964, Aalen). These Introductions have also been reprinted in vol. 1 of Green's own *Works* (1885).

   The modern photographic reprints are uncorrected: for instance, they retain the startling misquotation (p. 187, footnote) '*Does it contain any experimental reasoning concerning matter of fact and resistance?*'

3. The main exceptions, up to 1900, are:
   Thos. Brown, *Observations on the Nature and Tendency of the Doctrine of Mr. Hume, Concerning the Relation of Cause and Effect* (1804)
   [F. Palgrave], 'Hume and his Influence upon History', *Quarterly Review* 73, 536–92 (1844; repr. 1922 in Palgrave's *Collected Works*, vol. 9, Cambridge)
   J. H. Burton, *Life and Correspondence of David Hume*, 2 vols. (1846; repr. 1967, New York)
   J. F. Stephen, 'Hume's Essays', *Saturday Rev.* (1863; repr. 1892 in his *Horae Sabbaticae*, Second Series, London & New York)
   T. H. Grose, 'History of the Editions', in the *Philosophical Works*, vol. III, 15–84 (1874)

L. Stephen, *History of English Thought in the Eighteenth Century*, esp. vol. 1, ch. 6 (1876; repr. 1949, New York)

T. H. Huxley, *Hume* (1879) (Also in vol. 6 of his *Collected Essays*, 1894) (repr. 1968, New York)

R. Adamson, 'Hume, David', *Encycl. Britannica* (9th edn) vol. 12, 346–53 (1881)

J. H. Stirling, 'Kant has *not* answered Hume', *Mind* (Old Series) 9, 531–47 (1884)

W. Knight, *Hume* (1886)

L. A. Selby-Bigge, editions of *Treatise* (1888) and *Enquiries* (1894)

L. Stephen, 'Hume, David', in *Dict. Nat. Biog.* 28, 215–26 (1891)

H. A. Aikins, *The Philosophy of Hume* (1893, repr. 1976)

J. Bonar, *Philosophy and Political Economy* . . ., bk. 2, ch. 6 (1893)

W. B. Elkin, 'The Relation of the Treatise . . . (Book 1) to the Inquiry . . .', *Phil. Rev.* (1894)

E. Albee, 'Hume's Ethical System', ibid. (1897) (included in ch. 5 of his *History of English Utilitarianism*, 1902)

H. Calderwood, *David Hume* (1898)

4. The main writings on Hume of the period 1900–1924 are listed on pp. 17–26.

5. In two articles entitled 'The Naturalism of Hume'. These are included almost verbatim in his *Philosophy of David Hume* (1941), chs. 4, 5 (with appendix), and 6; they are also reprinted in *The Credibility of Divine Existence: The Collected Papers of Norman Kemp Smith*, edited by Porteous, Maclennan and Davie (1967). Kemp Smith had previously appeared in print on Hume, with the old-fashioned view, in his *Studies in the Cartesian Philosophy* (1902), ch. 6.

6. G. E. Moore, 'Hume's Philosophy', *The New Quarterly* 1909 (repr. 1922 in his *Philosophical Studies*); a similar treatment is found in his lectures of 1910/11, which were first printed in 1953—see Moore 1953; C. D. Broad, 'Hume's Theory of the Credibility of Miracles', *PAS* 1916–17 (repr. in Sesonske & Fleming 1965); A. N. Whitehead, 'Uniformity and contingency', *PAS* 1922–3 (repr. 1961 in A. N. Whitehead, *The Interpretation of Science: Selected Essays*, ed. by A. H. Johnson).

7. The Russian, Polish, Serbo-Croat, Spanish and Japanese general books on Hume I have not seen (Narsky 1967; Jedynak 1974; Životič 1959; Rábade Romeo 1975; Doi 1937).

8. After writing this, I was delighted to find that Kemp Smith apparently used the term: Hume's 'entire philosophy, both theoretical and practical, is built around the view of Nature as having an authority which man has neither the right nor the power to challenge' (Kemp Smith 1941, p. 564).

9. For assessments of all these books, see the reviews in the journals. (References to the reviews are given, in square brackets, within the entries in the bibliography.)

10. About twice as much, in fact. This can be seen by comparing the two most closely equivalent records: Hall, *A Hume Bibliography, from 1930* (1971) and Hall & Woolhouse,

'Forty Years of Work on John Locke (1929–1969), A Bibliography', *Phil. Q.* 20 (1970), 258–68.

11. Editor's Introduction to the *Enquiries*, p. vii. The full context of these remarks—by the experienced editor of the *Treatise* as well as the *Enquiries*—runs: 'Hume's philosophic writings are to be read with great caution. His pages, especially those of the Treatise, are so full of matter, he says so many different things in so many different ways and different connexions, and with so much indifference to what he has said before, that it is very hard to say positively that he taught, or did not teach, this or that particular doctrine. He applies the same principles to such a great variety of subects that it is not surprising that many verbal, and some real inconsistencies can be found in his statements. He is ambitious rather than shy of saying the same thing in different ways, and at the same time he is often slovenly and indifferent about his words and formulae. This makes it easy to find all philosophies in Hume, or, by setting up one statement against another, none at all.'

12. Morrisroe has finally settled the question whether Hume read Berkeley: he has discovered a letter that shows Hume read the *Principles* while at Rheims, in the library of the Abbé Pluche. Pluche was the author of the highly-successful work *Le Spectacle de la Nature* (8 vols., 1732–50). The best modern account of him is by Camille Limoges in the *Dictionary of Scientific Biography*, vol. XI (New York 1975).
The question what use Hume made of the Berkeley he read has received some definite answers (e.g. Hall 1970), but deserves further attention. Many passages in Berkeley may be relevant to Hume. For example, did the following passage of Berkeley provide the original stimulus for Hume's thinking on the idea of necessary connexion?

> That Food nourishes, Sleep refreshes, and Fire warms us; that to sow in the Seed-time is the way to reap in the Harvest . . . we know, not by discovering any necessary Connexion between our Ideas, but only by the Observation of the settled Laws of Nature . . . (*Principles,* §31: quoted from the 2nd edn, 1734)

Also compare (for the examples only) Hume's remark, 'If we believe, that fire warms, or water refreshes, 'tis only because it costs us too much pains to think otherwise' (*Treatise*, p. 270). [Since writing this, I have noticed that Hacking (1975) also quotes the Berkeley passage, with the same idea.]

13. Two examples may suffice. 'According to the thesis of this book there is no difficulty in deciding, for the *Dialogues* illustrate clearly the relation of Hume to scepticism. Cleanthes is Hume.' (Laing 1932, p. 179). 'I shall contend that Philo, from start to finish, represents Hume; and that Cleanthes can be regarded as Hume's mouthpiece only in those passages in which he is explicitly agreeing with Philo, or in those other passages in which, while refuting Demea, he is also being used to prepare the way for one or other of Philo's independent conclusions.' (Kemp Smith 1935; 2nd edn, p. 59). Kemp Smith's position is actually more qualified than it seems: he has already stipulated (on the

previous page) that 'Hume's own teaching is not presented through any one of the characters; it is developed in and through the argument as a whole, something of his own beliefs being put into the mouths of all three.'

14. I am not implying that this was the end of the matter. Gaskin (1976, p. 306) concludes, *contra* Noxon, 'that Philo is Hume and that Philo does challenge the argument for design'; but Noxon (1976) again defends his position that 'none of Hume's characters speaks consistently for Hume'. At the same time, in 'Philo's Confession', W. A. Parent (1976) argues that 'we cannot appeal to Philo's turnabout as a reason for declining to identify him as Hume's mouthpiece', and in his other 1976 article goes all out to make the identification. On the other hand, Bricke (1975) claims, in an excellent article, that it is a 'fundamental mistake to assume that one of the characters . . . serves as the author's primary spokesman', and gives as one reason, that 'Hume is a much better philosopher than Philo'.

15. Boswell's dream of 9th January 1784:

Awaked after a very agreeable dream that I had found a Diary kept by David Hume, from which it appeared that though his vanity made him publish treatises of scepticism and infidelity, he was in reality a Christian and a very pious Man. He had, I imagined, quieted his mind by thinking that whatever he might appear to the World to show his talents, his religion was between God and his own conscience. (I cannot be sure if this thought was in sleep.) I thought I read some beautiful passages in his Diary. I am not certain whether I had this dream on thursday night or friday night. But after I awaked, it dwelt so upon my mind that I could not for some time perceive that it was only a fiction.

(*The Boswell Papers*, XVI, 20; quoted by Mossner, 1943, p. 186; and, with slight differences, 1954, p. 606.)

16. That there is this uncertainty about Hume in general, so that the question can be continually reopened, is shown by the fact that Stove (1976) can write as follows: 'That his philosophy *is* of a predominantly destructive character I take to be as obvious to Hume's readers now, even after the efforts of Professor Kemp Smith to portray it in an opposite light, as it always was before' (Livingston & King, p. 58). A valuable piece on the general interpretation of Hume is that by Robison (1973), entitled 'Hume's scepticism'.

17. What I have in mind here is the use of methods that could be applied systematically to elicit the meaning of the text. There may be such methods to hand, in the studies made of other philosophers, or in other fields entirely; or some could be invented. I have tried to make a start, by applying, to the section 'Of personal identity' in the *Treatise*, a method of eliciting the meaning of the text by comparing it closely with its main source, in Locke. This is not just haphazard source-hunting, and does not rely merely on the old device of tracking down the use of the same examples—a device which is shown to be very uncertain—but rests on finding similarities of wording: 'there is an important difference be-

Notes and References

18. Hume used to be subjected to a curious type of personal criticism on the ground of *insincerity* (which surely is nothing to do with philosophy). There is the finale of Taylor (1927), and some equally odd remarks of Prichard (1932), e.g. 'To my mind the *Treatise* is one of the most tedious of books, and close examination of it renders me not sceptical but angry . . . The further Hume gets the more he gets into difficulties, and the more he gets into difficulties the more we feel that he is only θέσιν διαφυλάττων and casting about for reasons for believing what he does not believe and yet on his own principles is bound to believe. . . . It could be wished that the student of philosophy could be spared all contact with Hume, and thereby the trouble of rooting out some of the more gratuitous forms of confusion common in philosophy.' After this, a most refreshing voice is that of Price (1940), who tries to account for Hume's lack of appeal to such earnest men (p. 3) and concludes, 'this attitude of systematic hostility and quasi-moral disapprobation was a most unfortunate one'.

19. As a reprint of the original, the Selby-Bigge edition of the *Treatise* has very few mistakes of wording. One of these (*conversation* for *conversion*, in the middle of p. 63) was reported by me (Hall 1974, p. 68); the rest are listed by Nidditch (1976, pp. 35–6), who gives corrigenda for the wording of Mossner's edition also (ibid., pp. 38–42), as part of his critique of the chief current editions (ibid., pp. 33–46).

But the possibility is worth considering, that there may be quite a few mistakes of wording in the original edition of the *Treatise*. Several probable mistakes have been noticed so far, of such a type that they are more likely to be author's than printer's errors. They are: on p. 213 (using Selby-Bigge page numbers) *uninterrupted* for *interrupted*, and on p. 258, *imperfect* for *improper* (von Leyden 1957); p. 255, line 1, *vegetables* for *animals* (Hall 1974, p. 69); p. 391, 5 lines up, *hatred* for *pride* (Owen 1975); p. 463, line 1, *judgments* for *actions* (Harrison 1976, p. 20). Surely more will come to light, but only by careful attention to the meaning. (The MS is lost; except for a fragment, which has been published (described in Mossner 1949; full out in Nidditch 1976).)

20. This could usefully be extended. I propose the following additions. Grammarian—it belongs to him to examine what qualities are entitled to the denomination of *virtue*, 610 (i.e. he is what is now called a philosopher). Grammatical—questions concerning personal identity are to be regarded as, rather than as philosophical, 262 (i.e. as what is now called philosophical, rather than as empirical). Liars, 86, 117, 121. Maxim, 6, 50, 60, 76, 78, 98, 131 [etc.]. Phaenomenon, 4, 5, 9, 35, 60, 69, 99 [etc.].

21. For example, by M. A. Stewart in *Philosophical Books* 18
(1977), 49–54. Another edition deserving a mention is that
by Pike (1970). The text in this follows the wording of the
first edition, of 1779; there is a long and useful discussion.
For those who want the first edition without modernisation
of style, Pike says (p. xxiii) that he has checked the text of the
Dialogues in Cohen, *Essential Works of David Hume* (1965),
against the first edition and 'found it to be without error or
alteration'.

22. The editor claims (p. 11) that, save for the replacement of
the long ess, and the omission of the side-notes, the edition
is 'virtually identical with the 1754 one'. This claim has not
been checked, so far as I know.

23. Seven copies of the *Abstract* have now come to light (Bevan
& Price 1970, Connon 1976). Other writings of Hume that
were published for the first time in the period under discussion are the review of Henry (Mossner 1942), the essay
on chivalry and modern honour (Mossner 1947), and the
important early memoranda (Mossner 1948).

24. Published twice yearly. The editor is John W. Davis, and
the address is Department of Philosophy, University of
Western Ontario, London, Ontario N6A 3K7, Canada.

25. Perhaps literally: on page 99, Mossner goes to the trouble of
telling us that La Flèche is '150 miles south-east of Paris',
and this glaring mistake remains uncorrected in the Claren-
don Press re-issue (1970). There are other annoying errors,
e.g. the inversion of Johnson and Hume at the end of page
393; and nothing is said of Robert Adam's connexion with
the 'monument' that Hume expressly asked for in his will.
The Mossner *Life* has been a little over-rated with regard to
accuracy and completeness. Nor does it always entirely
supersede Greig (1931).

26. Preferably to the philosophical works. If not a Concordance,
showing every occurrence of each principal word together
with its immediate context, then let us have at least a Word
Index, with each occurrence of a word located by a reference. These can now be produced by computer. Two recent
examples are L. Brandwood, *A Word Index to Plato* (Leeds:
W. S. Maney, 1976) and P. Cahné, *Index du discours de la
méthode de René Descartes* (Rome: Edizioni dell' Ateneo,
1977).

27. No one would deny that much of Russell is in the spirit of
Hume; but, as Ronald Jager points out,

> It is Kant's example . . . more than Hume's, that provides
> the deeper context for Russell's theory of knowledge.
> Russell was, especially in the early decades of his career,
> much more deeply read in Kant than in Hume, and he
> long thought of many of his problems as modern versions,
> made novel and soluble by his new logic, of Kantian
> problems: 'existence' is a prime example, mathematical
> truth is another. His books on Geometry, on Leibniz, and
> also *Principles of Mathematics*, *Principia Mathematica*, and
> *Problems of Philosophy* largely ignore Hume, and all deal
> extensively with Kant.

(*The Development of Russell's Philosophy*, 1972, p. 266)

Austin found him too readable, Wittgenstein not enough.
Thus Hampshire reports of Austin: 'The plausibility of
Descartes and, worst of all, of Hume were particular examples that he would quote. He distrusted their literary
skill, [etc.]' (*Proc. Arist. Soc.* 60 [1959/60], p. xiii).
Whereas Britton reports of Wittgenstein: 'As for Hume and Kant,
[according to Wittgenstein] it was all very well for me to
read them because I was not yet as experienced in philosophical thinking as he was: but he could not sit down and
read Hume—he knew far too much about the subject of
Hume's writings to find this anything but a torture.' (*The
Listener*, 16 June 1955: vol. 53, p. 1072/1). This is confirmed
by another witness: 'He never read more than a few pages of
Hume.' (G. E. M. Anscombe, *An Introduction to Wittgenstein's
Tractatus*, 1959, p. 12).

I have mainly in mind, of course, Hume's effect on Kant,
which presumably altered the course of philosophy. And
there is Reid too. And Bentham, who on reading Book III
of the *Treatise* immediately 'felt as if scales had fallen' from
his eyes.

But Hume's influence on English writers of his age who
were not philosophers is a matter of some interest—even
though it had no effect on philosophy—and should not be
neglected. In particular, Samuel Johnson seems to have
studied Hume more seriously than is generally realised, at
least on the subject of miracles. Johnson had learnt how to
apply the Humean argument (Noyes 1962; Noyes describes
Johnson's analogous argument about Canada—for which see
Boswell, *Life*, 14 July, 1763). When, on another occasion,
Boswell twitted him with using the Humean argument,
Johnson replied that he actually agreed with Hume on this:
'Hume, taking the proposition simply, is right'. He added,
as one might expect, 'But the Christian Revelation is not
proved by the miracles alone, but as connected with pro-
phecies and with the doctrines in confirmation of which they
were wrought' (*Boswell Papers*, XIII, 54; quoted by Mossner,
1943, p. 186).

And Gibbon, of course, read the *History*, just as Hume
did his [the first volume, 1776]. He reported on the experience in his *Memoirs* (p. 99, Bonnard edn.): 'the calm
philosophy, the careless inimitable beauties . . . often forced
me to close the volume, with a mixed sensation of delight
and despair'.

THE BIBLIOGRAPHY

•

Note on the Catalogue

The main part of the catalogue provides a record of the critical work on Hume published from 1925 to 1976. The works are listed in a single series, alphabetically by author within each year. Particulars should be found here of all the books and articles—in virtually all major languages—that either were devoted entirely to Hume or contained a substantial discussion of some aspect of his work or his life. (In the case of discussions, specific references to chapters or pages are normally given.)

References to selected reviews of the books on Hume, and to criticisms or discussions of any of the listed works, are also provided. These references are placed in square brackets, within the relevant entry; a discussion that appeared in a journal is usually given a full entry as well, under its own year. Dates and locations of reprintings of books are given, when informative; of articles and chapters, whenever known.

Dissertations have been included, usually with the names of the universities accepting them: they can normally be consulted in those institutions or obtained on loan or in microform. (Details of their content can often be discovered from *Dissertation Abstracts*.) However, I have not always troubled to record as such those dissertations that were subsequently published as books.

Also included in the listing are the new editions, collections and anthologies of Hume's own writings; but translations of Hume have normally been excluded, unless they are of special interest because of their introductory matter or annotations. Mere reprints of single works of Hume in general anthologies of philosophy have been disregarded.

THE MAIN WRITINGS ON HUME

1900–24

[1900]

GROOS, K. 'Hat Kant Humes *Treatise* gelesen ?', *Kant-Studien* 5, 177–81.

GROTE, J. *Exploratio Philosophica*, pt. 2, esp. bk. 1, ch. 5 ('Hume on the Origin of Ideas'). Cambridge.

HØFFDING, H. *A History of Modern Philosophy*, vol. 1, bk. 4, ch. 5. London.

HUSSERL, E. *Logische Untersuchungen*, Bd. 2, Untersuchung 2, Kap. 5 ('Phänomenologische Studie über Humes Abstraktionstheorie'). Halle. (Engl. transl. 1970 as *Logical Investigations*)

KLEMME, M. *Die volkswirtschaftlichen Anschauungen David Humes.* (v, 42 pp.) Halle (diss.).

KLEMME, M. *Die volkswirtschaftlichen Anschauungen David Hume's, ein Beitrag zur Geschichte der Volkswirtschaftslehre.* (viii, 100 pp.) Jena.

LECHARTIER, G. *David Hume, moraliste et sociologue.* (275 pp.) Paris.

SCOTT, W. R. *Francis Hutcheson: His life, teaching and position in the history of philosophy*, 115–30. Cambridge.

[1901]

GRAHAM, H. G. *Scottish Men of Letters in the Eighteenth Century*. London.

LINKE, P. *David Humes Lehre vom Wissen, ein Beitrag zur Relationstheorie im Anschluss an Locke und Hume.* (55 pp.) Leipzig (diss.).

LINKE, P. 'Hume's Lehre vom Wissen', *Philosophische Studien* 17, 624–73.

LÜERS, A. *David Humes religionsphilosophische Anschauungen.* (21 pp.) Berlin (diss.).

PREHN, A. *Die Bedeutung der Einbildungskraft bei Hume und Kant für die Erkenntnistheorie.* Halle (diss.).

REININGER, R. 'Das Causalproblem bei Hume und Kant', *Kant-Studien* 6, 427–58.
VAN MELLE, M. A. *David Hume en zijne leer van het kenvermogen.* Amsterdam.

[**1902**]

ALBEE, E. *A History of English Utilitarianism,* ch. 5 (a reprint of his 1897 article in *Phil. Rev.,* with an added section on pp. 107–10) London. (repr. 1957)
DELACROIX, H. 'David Hume et la philosophie critique', *Bibliothèque du Congrès internationale de Philosophie* 4, (*Histoire de la Philosophie*). Paris.
GORE, W. C. *The Imagination in Spinoza and Hume.* (77 pp.) Chicago.
[KEMP] SMITH, N. *Studies in the Cartesian Philosophy,* ch. 6. London.
MARCUS, E. *Kants Revolutionsprinzip* (Kopernikanisches Prinzip). *Eine exakte Lösung des Kant-Hume'schen Erkenntnisproblems* . . . (xii, 181 pp.) Herford.
MIRKIN, I. 'Hat Kant Hume widerlegt ?', *Kant-Studien* 7, 230–99.
SCHATZ, A. *L'Oeuvre économique de David Hume.* (xii, 303 pp.) Paris. (repr. 1972, New York)
SNOW, L. F. 'The Education of David Hume', *Sewanee Rev.* 10, 207–22.
TEISSEIRE, M. *Les Essais économiques de David Hume.* (214 pp.) Paris.

[**1903**]

ADAMSON, R. *The Development of Modern Philosophy,* pt. 2, ch. 3. Edinburgh. (repr. 1908)
ALIOTTA, A. *Scetticismo antico e scetticismo moderno.* Piacenza.
APPELDOORN, J. G. *De leer der sympathie bij Hume en Adam Smith.* Amsterdam.
DAICHES, Sally. *Über das Verhältnis der Geschichtsschreibung D. Hume's zu seiner praktischen Philosophie.* (59 pp.) Leipzig (diss.).
FALTER, L. *Die erkenntnistheoretischen Grundlagen der Mathematik bei Kant und Hume.* (72 pp.) Giessen (diss.).
GOLDSTEIN, J. *Die empiristische Geschichtsauffassung David Humes.* . . . Leipzig.

McGILVARY, E. B. 'Altruism in Hume's *Treatise*', *Phil. Rev.* 12, 272–98.

OHLENDORF, H. L. *Hume's Affektenlehre.* (iv, 107 pp.) Erlangen (diss.).

ORR, James. *David Hume and his Influence on Philosophy and Theology.* (ix, 246 pp.) Edinburgh.

QUAST, O. *Der Begriff des Belief bei David Hume.* (viii, 125 pp.) Halle.

ZIMELS, J. *David Humes Lehre vom Glauben und ihre Entwickelung vom 'Treatise' zur 'Inquiry'.* (84 pp.) Berlin.

[1904]

COOK, E. A. *Hume's Theorie über die Realität der Aussenwelt.* (43 pp.) Halle (diss.).

ELKIN, W. B. *Hume: The Relation of the Treatise of Human Nature—Book I, to the Inquiry Concerning Human Understanding* [based on results partly published in *Phil. Rev.* 3 (1894)] (ix, 330 pp.) New York & London.

FEIGS, A. *Die Begriffe der Existenz, Substanz und Kausalität bei Hume.* (62 pp.) Waldenburg i. Schl. (diss.).

HÖNIGSWALD, R. *Über die Lehre Hume's von der Realität der Aussendinge.* (viii, 88 pp.) Berlin (diss.).

NATHANSOHN, H. *Der Existenzbegriff Hume's.* (75 pp.) Berlin (diss.).

RICHTER, R. *Der Skeptizismus in der Philosophie,* 2 vols. Leipzig. (vol. 2, 1908)

STEIN, L. 'Hat Kant Hume widerlegt ?', *Zukunft* 12.

[1905]

GERBER, F. *Über das Verhältnis von Wahrnehmung und Vorstellung unter sich und zur subjektiven Wirklichkeit mit besonderer Berücksichtigung von Hume und Berkeley.* (97 pp.) Leipzig (diss.).

[KEMP] SMITH, N. 'The Naturalism of Hume', *Mind* 14, 149–73 and 335–47. (for reprintings, see note 5 preceding)

MARTIN, John J. *Shaftesbury's und Hutcheson's Verhältnis zu Hume.* (124 pp.) Halle (diss.).

MONTAGUE, W. P. 'A Neglected Point in Hume's Philosophy', *Phil. Rev.* 14, 30–9.

RAFFEL, F. *Englische Freihändler vor Adam Smith.* (v, 193 pp.) (*Zeitschrift für die gesamte Staatswissenschaft,* Ergänzungsheft 18.) Tübingen.

RUIE, C. *Materialism as a Philosophical Conception of the Universe, or Hume vindicated.* (xv, 150 pp.) Montreal.
VINOGRADOV, N. D. Философія Давида Юма. Часть 1-я: Теоретическая философія Д. Юма. (260 pp.) Moscow.

[1906]

GOPCSA, E. 'Hume véleménye az ok és okozat között való viszonyról' (Hume's opinion on the relation between cause and effect), *Bölcseleti Folyóirat*, 1–28.
HEDVALL, C. *Humes Erkenntnistheorie kritisch dargestellt.* (129 pp.) Uppsala.
LOVEJOY, A. 'On Kant's Reply to Hume', *Arch. Gesch. Phil.*, Neue Folge 12, 380–407.
MÜLLER, Felix. *David Humes Stellung zum Deismus.* (53 pp.) Leipzig (diss.).
RICKABY, J. J. *Free Will and Four English Philosophers* (*Hobbes, Locke, Hume and Mill*), 115–62. London. (repr. 1969, Freeport, N.Y.)
SABINE, G. H. 'Hume's Contribution to the Historical Method', *Phil. Rev.* 15, 17–38.
SCHILLER, F. C. S. 'Humism and Humanism', *Proc. Arist. Soc.* 7, 93–111. (repr. 1912 in his *Humanism*)
WITIES, B. 'Humes Theorie der Leichtgläubigkeit der Menschen . . .', *Arch. syst. Phil.* 12.

[1907]

ARNOLDT, E. 'Wie erfasste Kant das Humesche Problem ?', in *Gesammelte Schriften*, Nachlass, Bd. 3.
FRANCKEN, C. J. W. *David Hume.* (viii, 147 pp.) Haarlem.
SÖHRING, O. 'David Humes "Skeptizismus"', *Philosophische Wochenschrift* 7 (1907) and 8 (1908).
SOPPER, A. J. de. *David Hume's Kenleer en Ethiek. Eerste, inleidend deel: Van Bacon tot Hume.* (xi, 200 pp.) Leiden. (no more published)
STÖRRING, O. *David Hume's Skeptizismus, ein Weg zur Philosophie.* Schönenberg.
SUSSNITZKI, I. *Die Gesellschafts- und Staatslehre David Humes.* (viii, 101 pp.) Strasbourg (diss.).
WALZ, W. E. *David Humes Verhältnis zur Erkenntnislehre Lockes und Berkeleys.* (vi, 43 pp.) Tübingen (diss.).

JOFFE, A. 'Die Philosophie des Individualismus und die bürgerliche Gesellschaft: Hume und Mach', *Die Neue Zeit* 26.

NEUHAUS, C. *Humes Lehre von den Prinzipien der Ethik* ... (v, 55 pp.) Leipzig (diss.).

SCHWENNINGER, A. *Der Sympathiebegriff bei David Hume.* ... (51 pp.) Munich (diss.).

[1909]

BÖHME, A. *Die Wahrscheinlichkeitslehre bei David Hume.* (45 pp.) Berlin.

BULLIAT, G. *Réfutations des objections de Hume et de Kant contre l'analytique du principe de causalité.* (U. of California Publications in Philosophy.)

KAYSERLING, H. *Die Willenstheorie bei John Locke und David Hume.* (79 pp.) Place not given (diss.).

LÉVY-BRUHL, L. 'L'orientation de la pensée philosophique de David Hume', *Revue Mét.* 17, 595–619.

MOORE, G.E. 'Hume's Philosophy', *New Q.* 2, 545–65. (repr. 1922 in his *Philosophical Studies*, and 1949 in Feigl & Sellars, *Readings in Philosophical Analysis*; a similar treatment is in Moore 1953, originally lectures given in 1910–11)

NEUHAUS, K. 'Humes Lehre von den Prinzipien der Ethik', *Z. Phil.* 135. (cf. Neuhaus 1908)

RÖDDER, P. *Über Humes Erkenntnistheorie.* (11 pp.) Gollnow.

THOMSEN, A. 'David Hume's *Natural History of Religion*', *The Monist* 19, 269–88.

WALZ, E. 'David Humes Beurteilung in der Geschichte der Philosophie', *Philosophisches Jahrbuch* 22.

WÜST, P. 'Zu Theodor Lipps' Neuausgabe seiner deutschen Bearbeitung von Humes *Treatise* ...', *Kant-Studien* 14, 249–73.

[1910]

BILHARZ, A. *Descartes, Hume und Kant. Eine kritische Studie zur Geschichte der Philosophie.* (78 pp.) Wiesbaden.

BOLCEWICZ, H. 'Stosunek Hume'a i Kanta do metafizyki w tym samym zbiorze', *Szkice Filozoficzne, Księga Pamiątkowa ku czci Prof. Maurycego Straszewskiego*, 77–89. Cracow.

COURTOIS, L.-J. 'Le Séjour de ... Rousseau en Angleterre' [with unpub. letters of Hume], *Ann. Soc. J.-J. Rousseau* 16.

DETMAR, B. *Karneades und Hume.* (57 pp.) Berlin (diss.). Also in *Z. Phil.* 139 (1910) 113–57.

SĘKOWSKI, F. 'Czy "ideje" Hume'a są kopią "impresji" ?',
Szkice Filozoficzne, Księga Pam. M. Straszewskiego. Cracow.

WALZ, E. 'David Hume und der Positivismus und
Nominalismus', *Philosophisches Jahrbuch* 23, 161–82.

[**1911**]

ADAMSON, R. & MITCHELL, J. M. 'Hume, David', in
Encyclopaedia Britannica, 11th edn (vol. 13, pp. 876–84).
New York.

FUETER, E. *Geschichte der neueren Historiographie.* Munich.
(French transl. 1914: see below)

HEIN, J. 'Humes Kausaltheorie verglichen mit derjenigen
Kants', *Philosophisches Jahrbuch* 24, 48–70.

HUDSON, J. W. *The Treatment of Personality by Locke, Berkeley
and Hume.* (xvi, 100 pp.) Columbia, Missouri.

LINDSAY, A. D. Introductions (vii–xxvi, and vii–xv) to
David Hume, A Treatise of Human Nature. 2 vols.
(Everyman's Library) London & New York.

PETRESCU, N. *Glanvill und Hume.* (71 pp.) Berlin.
[*JHI* 14 (1953) 294]

REINACH, A. 'Kants Auffassung des Humeschen Problems',
Z. Phil. 141, 176–209. (repr. 1921 in his *Gesammelte Schriften*,
Halle) (transl. as Reinach 1976)

SALINGER, R. *Humes Kritik des Kausalbegriffs und ihre
erkenntnistheoretische Bedeutung.* Berlin.

THOMSEN, A. *David Hume, hans Liv og hans Filosofi.* (iv,
458 pp.) Copenhagen. (German transl. 1912: see below)

VALCHERA, L. *David Hume e la sua influenza nel campo sociale.*
(57 pp.) Frosinone.

[**1912**]

DIDIER, J. *David Hume.* Paris.

LÉVY-BRUHL, L. 'Quelques Mots sur la Querelle de Hume et
de Rousseau', *Revue Mét.* 20, 417–28.

MÜNSTER, O. *Det Hume'ske Problem.* [A criticism of Thomsen
1911] (67 pp.) Copenhagen.

SETH, J. *English Philosophers and Schools of Philosophy*, pt. 2,
ch. 2. London.

STOCK, St. G. *English Thought for English Thinkers*, ch. 4.
London.

THOMSEN, A. *David Hume, sein Leben und seine Philosophie.*
[transl. of the Danish book of 1911] Berlin.

BOLCEWICZ, H. *Kant a Hume*. (103 pp.) Warsaw.

CASAZZA, G. *Hume, Kant e lo scetticismo filosofico*. (viii, 132 pp.) Rome & Milan.

DOODKORTE, A. C. *Kritiek op David Hume: Over natuurwet en wonder*. Bussum.

FIRTH, C. H. 'The Development of the Study of Seventeenth-Century History', *Trans. R. hist. Soc.*, ser. 3, vol. 7, 25–48 (pp. 38–9 are on Hume).

HUNT, W. 'Hume and Modern Historians', in *The Cambridge History of English Literature*, vol. 10, ch. 12. Cambridge.

ROSENFELD, J. 'Die doppelte Wahrheit, mit besonderer Rücksicht auf Leibniz und Hume', *Berner Studien Phil.* 75.

RUDAJEW, M.-B. *Mach und Hume*. (Heidelberg, diss.) Berlin.

SORLEY, W. R. 'David Hume', in *The Cambridge History of English Literature*, vol. 10, ch. 14, 321–35. Cambridge. (repr. 1920 as ch. 8 of his *History of British Philosophy*)

WOODBRIDGE, F. J. E. 'Hume', in James Hastings, *Encyclopaedia of Religion and Ethics*, vol. 6 (867/1–870/1). Edinburgh, etc.

ALBERT, F. *Das Verhältnis Herbert Spencers zu David Hume in der Erkenntnistheorie*. Leipzig (diss.).

BAUCH, B. 'Parallelstellen bei Hume und Kant', *Kant-Studien* 19, 521–3.

FAHRION, K. *Humes Lehre von der Substanz*. (31 pp.) Ellwangen.

FUETER, E. *Histoire de l'historiographie moderne*, 452–6. Paris. (transl. of 1911 German original)

LAMB, F. J. ' "Studies in Theology" and Hume's "Essay on Miracles" ', *Bibliotheca Sacra* 71, 105–31.

LAUER, C. *Der Irrationalismus als philosophischer Grundzug David Humes*. (95 pp.) Berlin.

MEINICKE, M. *Die Wurzeln der Religion im menschlichen Gemüt nach David Hume* . . . Eisenach.

PHALÉN, A. K. *Humes psykologiska härledning av kausalitets-föreställningen*. Uppsala & Stockholm. (transl. 1977 as 'Hume's Psychological Explanation of the Idea of Causality', *Int. phil. Q.* 17, 43–57)

DE MICHELIS, E. 'Su le dottrine sociologiche e politiche di
David Hume', in *Studi di storia e di critica dedicati a O. C.
Falletti*. Bologna.

KEMP SMITH, N. 'Kant's Relation to Hume and to Leibnitz',
Phil. Rev. 24, 288–96. (repr. 1918 as ch. 2 of his
Commentary to Kant's Critique of Pure Reason)

SHEARER, E. A. *Hume's Place in Ethics*. (Bryn Mawr, diss.).
Baltimore.

THORMEYER, P. *Die grossen englischen Philosophen Locke,
Berkeley, Hume*. Leipzig.

ZURKUHLEN, H. *Berkeleys und Humes Stellung zur Analysis des
Unendlichen*. (103 pp.) Berlin (diss.).

[1916]

BOHN, W. *Leibniz und Hume als Erkenntnistheoretiker*.
Bonn (diss.).

BROAD, C. D. 'Hume's Theory of the Credibility of Miracles',
Proc. Arist. Soc. 17, 77–94. (repr. 1965 in Sesonske &
Fleming, *Human Understanding*)

DOXSEE, C. W. 'Hume's Relation to Malebranche', *Phil. Rev.*
25, 692–710.

WARREN, H. C. 'Mental association from Plato to Hume',
Psychol. Rev. 23, 208–30. (repr. 1921 as ch. 2 of his *History
of the Association Psychology*, New York; repr. 1967)

[1917]

[ANON.] 'Hume's Suppressed Essays', *Open Court* 31,
740–56. (repr. of the essays on suicide and immortality)

HENDEL, C. W. *Studies in the philosophy of David Hume*.
(420 pp.) Princeton U. (diss.).

SETH PRINGLE-PATTISON, A. *The Idea of God, in the light of
recent philosophy*, Lecture I. Oxford.

[1918]

KEMP SMITH, N. *A Commentary to Kant's Critique of Pure
Reason*, Introduction, ch. 2, 'Kant's Relation to Hume and to
Leibniz' [a reprint of his 1915 article]; and Appendix B.
London. (2nd edn 1923; repr. 1930; repr. 1962, New York)

HASSE, H. *Das Problem der Gültigkeit in der Philosophie David Humes.* (193 pp.) Leipzig. (repr. 1920, Munich)

[**1920**]

MERLEKER, M. *Humes Begriff der Realität.* (v, 109 pp.) Halle.
SORLEY, W. R. *A History of British Philosophy to 1900,* ch. 8.
[A reprint of his 1913 chapter in the *Cambridge History of English Literature*] Cambridge. (repr. 1965)

[**1921**]

PASTORE, A. *Il problema della causalità.* Turin.
PETZOLD, A. *Hume und Lipps in der Assoziationspsychologie.* Erlangen (diss.).
POSEN, E. *Die 'Existenz' bei David Hume.* (56 pp.) Giessen (diss.).
SHARP, F. C. 'Hume's Ethical Theory and Its Critics', *Mind* 30, 40–56 and 151–71.
TAYLOR, A. E. 'Theism', sec. 14, in James Hastings, *Encyclopaedia of Religion and Ethics,* vol. 12. Edinburgh, etc.

[**1922**]

BRÜSSOW, L. *Die Auffassung von Einbildungskraft und Verstand und ihr gegenseitiges Verhältnis bei Hume, Kant und Fichte.* Greifswald (diss.).
REININGER, R. *Locke, Berkeley, Hume.* (*Geschichte der Philosophie in Einzeldarstellungen,* Bd. 22 / 3) Munich.
WENTSCHER, E. *Geschichte des Kausalproblems in der neueren Philosophie,* ch. 7, sec. 3. Leipzig.
WHITEHEAD, A. N. 'Uniformity and contingency', *Proc. Arist. Soc.* 23, 1–18. (repr. 1961 in Whitehead, *The Interpretation of Science: Selected Essays,* ed. by A. H. Johnson, Indianapolis & New York)

[**1923**]

HÖNIGSWALD, R. *Geschichte der Philosophie von der Renaissance bis Kant.* Berlin & Leipzig.
LEVI, A. 'David Hume e la critica del pensiero religioso', *Riv. Fil.* 14.

MORROW, G.R. 'The Significance of the Doctrine of Sympathy in Hume and Adam Smith', *Phil. Rev.* 32, 60–78.

[**1924**]

DUCASSE, C. J. *Causation and the Types of Necessity*, ch. 1 ('Hume'). Seattle. (repr. 1969, New York)
FAGGI, A. 'David Hume e Magalotti', *Atti della R. Accad. delle scienze di Torino* 59, 348–52.

THE HUME LITERATURE

1925-76

[1925]

BRAHAM, E. G. *The Problem of the Self and Immortality*, ch. 2, pt. B (67–91). London.

BROAD, C. D. *The Mind and its Place in Nature*, esp. ch. 3. London. [*JP* 24 (1927) 29–36]

EVTHIMY, S. Учението на Давидъ Юмъ за съчувствието — симпатията — и паралелъ между него и Т. Липсовото учение за 'вчувствуванието'. (With a German summary and a German title: Die Sympathielehre von David Hume und die Parallele zwischen ihr und der Einfühlungslehre von Theodor Lipps.) (63 pp.) Sofia.

FOLKIERSKI, W. *Entre le classicisme et le romantisme*, 46–52. Cracow & Paris.

HELLSTRÖM, C. F. A. *Om Hume's Aprioribegrepp*. (60 pp.) (*Uppsala Universitets Årsskrift*, vol. 1) Uppsala.

HENDEL, C. W. *Studies in the Philosophy of David Hume*. Princeton. (2nd edn Indianapolis 1963: see 1963) [*M*34 (1925) 379–82; *J P*22 (1925) 411–18; *PR*35 (1926) 483–6; *KS* 32 (1927) 373–4]

LAMPRECHT, S. P. 'Empiricism and Epistemology in David Hume', in *Studies in the History of Ideas* 2, ed. by Dept. of Philosophy, Columbia U., 221–52. New York.

MAZZANTINI, C. 'L'errore metafisico di David Hume', *Riv. Fil. neo-scolastica* 18, 162–77.

MURE, B. G. 'Some Unpublished Letters of David Hume', *Nineteenth Century* 98, 293–306.

POTTLE, F. A. 'The part played by Horace Walpole and James Boswell in the quarrel between Rousseau and Hume', *Philol. Q.* 4, 351–63. (cf. 1967 Pottle)

RADAKOVIC, K. *Die letzten Fundamente der Humeschen Erkenntnistheorie*. (53 pp.) Graz.

TVRDÝ, J. *Problém skutečnosti u Davida Huma a jeho význam v dějinách filosofie*. (90 pp.) Brno.

VAUGHAN, C. E. *Studies in the History of Political Philosophy before and after Rousseau*, vol. 1, ch. 6 (303–64: 'The Assault on Contract'). Manchester. (repr. 1960, New York)

[1926]

BLACK, J. B. *The Art of History: A study of four great historians of the eighteenth century*, 77–116. London. (repr. 1965, New York)

CARLINI, A. 'L'attualismo scettico del Trattato ... di D. Hume', in his edn of *Trattato sull'intelletto umano*, 341–76. Bari. (also in *G. crit. Fil. ital.* 7, 104–28)

DEHN, F. *Die Ethik David Humes.* (32 pp.) Bonn (diss.).

ELLIOTT, P. P. *Arguments for theism from design in nature with special reference to Hume, Paley, and Kant*. Oxford U. (diss.).

GENT, W. *Die Philosophie des Raumes und der Zeit*, ch. 50 (233–42). Bonn.

LAING, B. M. 'David Hume and the Contemporary Theory of Instinct', *The Monist* 36, 645–66.

LIBERTINI, C. *Il principio della morale in David Hume*. Naples.

METZ, R. 'Berkeley und Hume. 2. Teil: Hume', *Literarische Berichte aus dem Gebiete der Philosophie*, Heft 11 / 12, 24–9.

WEGRICH, A. D. *Die Geschichtsauffassung David Humes im Rahmen seines philosophischen Systems*. Cologne (diss.).

[1927]

ALLAN, D. M. 'Personal Agency and the Humian Analysis', *J. Phil.* 24, 645–56.

BARLINGAY, D. S. *Philosophical atomism: a comparative study of the theories of Hume and Bertrand Russell*. London (diss.).

GÜNTZBERG, B. 'Dawid Hume i teoria umowy społecznej', *Kwartalnik Filozoficzny*, 185–227 and 280–327.

HENDEL, C. W. *Hume, Selections*. New York, etc.

HOERNLÉ, R. F. A. 'Broad and Hume on Causation and Volition', *J. Phil.* 24, 29–36. (on Broad 1925)

SCHINZ, A. 'La Querelle Rousseau-Hume. Un document inédit', *Ann. Soc. J.-J. Rousseau* 17, 13–48.

TAYLOR, A. E. *David Hume & the Miraculous.* (The Leslie Stephen Lecture) Cambridge. (repr. 1934 in Taylor, *Phil. Studies*; also 1972, Folcroft Library Editions)
[*P*3 (1928) 535–7; Greig 1931, 162–3; Flew 1961, ch. 8]

CHAPMAN, R. W. 'Hume's Essays', let. to *TLS* (7 June) 431.
[*TLS* (1 Jan. 1971) 15; Colver 1974]

ECKSTEIN, W. 'Ein unveröffentlichter Brief David Humes',
Engl. Studien 62, 461–2.

ELTON, O. *A Survey of English Literature, 1730–1780*, vol. 2,
159–69 and 272–7. London.

MACH, F. 'Prawidło smaku według rozprawy D. Hume'a pt.
"Standard of Taste"', *Przeglad Filozoficzny*, 171–4.

METZ, R. 'Bibliographie der Hume-Literatur', *Literarische
Berichte aus dem Gebiete der Philosophie*, Heft 15 / 16, 39–50.

PELIKÁN, F. *Fikcionalism novovověké filosofie zvláště u Humea a
Kanta.* (208 pp.) Prague.

PEOPLES, M. H. 'La Querelle Rousseau-Hume', *Ann. Soc.
J.-J. Rousseau* 18, 1–331. Geneva.

ANNAND, M. R. *The treatment of relations by Locke and Hume.*
London (diss.).

BORING, E. G. *A History of Experimental Psychology*, esp.
186–95. New York.

BRENTANO, F. *Vom Dasein Gottes*, secs. 21–4. Hamburg.

GUNN, J. A. *The Problem of Time*, 79–86. London.

LAIRD, J. *The Idea of Value*, ch. 6, sec. 4. Cambridge.

LEROY, A.-L. *La critique et la religion chez David Hume.*
(xix, 376 pp.) Paris. (no date given)
[*JP* 29 (1932) 243–7; *PR* 43 (1934) 421–9]

METZ, R. *David Hume: Leben und Philosophie.* Stuttgart.
(repr. 1968, Stuttgart-Bad Cannstatt)
[*M* 39 (1930) 226–30; *KS* 35 (1930) 322–5]

METZ, R. 'Unveröffentlichte Briefe David Humes',
Engl. Studien 63, 337–88.

METZ, R. 'Les amitiés françaises de Hume et le mouvement des
idées', *Revue Litt. comp.* 9, 644–713.

MILLER, H. 'The Naturalism of Hume', *Phil. Rev.* 38, 469–82.

SALMON, C. V. 'The Central Problem of David Hume's
Philosophy: an essay towards a phenomenological
interpretation of the first book of the *Treatise* . . .', *Jahrbuch
für Phil. und Phänomenol. Forschung* 10. (151 pp.) Halle.
[*JP* 27 (1930) 575–9; *M* 39 (1930) 240–2; *KS* 35 (1930)
326–9]

SWANN, G. R. *Philosophical Parallelisms in Six English Novelists*,
ch. 4 ('Fielding and Empirical Realism'). Philadelphia:
U. of Pennsylvania (diss.). (repr. 1969, Folcroft, Pa.)

THIES, H. *David Hume als wirtschaftlicher und politischer Schriftsteller.* Cologne (diss.).

TOYNBEE, P. 'Mme du Deffand and Hume', *Mod. Lang. Rev.* 24, 447–51.

WHITEHEAD, A. N. *Process and Reality*, passim. Cambridge.

WINCKLER, C. *David Hume, Untersuchungen über die Prinzipien der Moral.* Leipzig. (last repr. 1972, Hamburg)
[*KS* 35 (1930) 319–20]

[1930]

ANNAND, M. R. 'An Examination of Hume's Theory of Relations', *The Monist* 40, 581–97. (also *Calcutta Rev.*, 16–30).

BONAR, J. *Moral Sense*, chs. 7–8 (121–67). London & New York.

BROAD, C. D. *Five Types of Ethical Theory*, ch. 4. London. (repr. 1976 in J. Glickman, *Moral Philosophy: An introduction*, New York)

HOBART, R. E. (= MILLER, D. S.) 'Hume without scepticism', *Mind* 39, 273–301 and 409–25.

KERR, S. A. *Hume's doctrine of imagination.* Oxford U. (diss.)

KUYPERS, M. S. *Studies in the Eighteenth-Century Background of Hume's Empiricism.* Minneapolis. (repr. 1966, New York)
[*JP* 28 (1931) 585–6]

LAIRD, J. *Knowledge, Belief and Opinion*, chs. 2 and 5. London & New York. (repr. 1972, Hamden, Conn.)

LEHMANN, W. C. *Adam Ferguson and the Beginnings of Modern Sociology*, 197–205. New York.

SAUER, F. 'Über das Verhältnis der Husserlschen Phänomenologie zu David Hume', *Kant-Studien* 35, 151–82.

WELDON, J. M. *The treatment of causality in the philosophy of Hume.* Nat. U. of Ireland (diss.).

[1931]

BONAR, J. *Theories of Population from Raleigh to Arthur Young*, ch. 6 (163–90). London. (repr. 1966, New York)

BRAHAM, E. G. *The Life of David Hume (the terrible David).* (99 pp.) London.

DELLA VOLPE, G. *La teoria delle passioni di Davide Hume.* Bologna. [*P* 7 (1932) 348]

GREIG, J. Y. T. *David Hume.* (436 pp.) London. (repr. 1954)
[*JP* 30 (1933) 81–3]

JOHNSON, E. A. J. 'L'économie synthétique de Hume',
  Revue d'hist. écon. et soc. 19, 225–43. (repr. 1937 in English in
  Johnson, *Predecessors* . . ., as ch. 9)
MEYERSON, E. *Du cheminement de la pensée*, vol. 2, secs. 317–27.
  Paris.
MORRIS, C. R. *Locke, Berkeley, Hume*, 108–58. London.
  [*P* 6 (1931) 391–2; *JP* 28 (1931) 664–6]
STOUT, G. F. *Mind & Matter*, esp. 22–33 (in ch. 2, 'The
  Animistic View of Causal Process'). Cambridge. [Ayer 1940]
STRACHEY, Lytton. *Portraits in Miniature*, 141–53. London.
TATARKIEWICZ, W. *Historia Filozofii*. Lwów. (6th edn,
  Warsaw 1968)
WENTSCHER, E. *Englische Wege zu Kant*, ch. 9 (69–84).
  Leipzig.

[**1932**]

DAWES HICKS, G. *Berkeley*, 252–68. London. (repr. 1968,
  New York)
DICKSON, W. K. 'David Hume and the Advocates' Library',
  Jurid. Rev. 44, 1–14. (repr. 1932 separately [16 pp.],
  Edinburgh)
GREIG, J. Y. T. 'Some unpublished letters to David Hume',
  Revue Litt. comp. 12, 826–56.
GREIG, J. Y. T. *The Letters of David Hume.* 2 vols. Oxford.
  (repr. 1969)
  [*M* 42 (1933) 523–8; *Yale Rev.* 23 (1933) 188–90]
GREIG, J. Y. T. & BEYNON, H. 'Calendar of Hume MSS. in the
  Possession of the Royal Society of Edinburgh'. (Issued
  separately 20 Jan. 1932) *Proc. R. Soc. Edinb.* 52, pt. 1 (1–138).
JOAD, C. E. M. 'Hume, David', in E. R. A. Seligman &
  A. Johnson, *Encyclopedia of the Social Sciences* (vol. 7, 550–2).
  New York.
KYD, G. O. *The Scottish answer to Hume.* Oxford U. (diss.).
LAING, B. M. *David Hume.* London. (repr. 1968, New York)
  [*P* 8 (1933) 220–5 (Ryle)]
LAIRD, J. *Hume's Philosophy of Human Nature.* London.
  (repr. 1967, Hamden, Conn.)
  [*P* 7 (1932) 357–60; *JP* 30 (1933) 128–36; *KS* 38 (1933)
  437–8; *M* 42 (1933) 67–75; *PR* 43 (1934) 212–13]
MACE, C. A. 'Hume's Doctrine of Causality', *Proc. Arist. Soc.*
  32, 301–28. (repr. 1973 in his *Selected Papers*)
PRICHARD, H. A. *Knowledge and Perception* (1950), 174–99.
  Oxford. [*Noûs* 1 (1967) 274–7]

TEGEN, E. *Humes uppfattning av jagets identitet.* (32 pp.,
with German summary) Uppsala, etc.
WIND, E. 'Humanitätsidee und heroisiertes Porträt in der
englischen Kultur des 18. Jahrhunderts', *Vorträge der
Bibliothek Warburg*, hsg. von Fritz Saxl, 156–229.
Leipzig & Berlin.
ZIMMERN, H. *Schopenhauer*, 96–7. London.
ZINI, Z. 'Rousseau e Hume', *Cultura*, 695–725.

[**1933**]

BERKOVITS, L. *Hume und der Deismus.* Berlin (diss.).
DAL VERME, M. E. 'Osservazioni sul concetto di miracolo
in Hume', *Riv. Fil. neo-scolastica* 25, 159–63.
DELLA VOLPE, G. *La filosofia dell'esperienza di Davide Hume.*
2 vols. (vol. 2, 1935). Florence. (2nd edn 1939; repr. 1973,
Rome) [*KS* 40 (1935) 304–5; *CC* 88 (1937) 53–60]
DE MICHELIS, E. 'David Hume e il problema critico della
conoscenza nella filosofia moderna', *Riv. Fil.* 24, 285–309.
LAPORTE, J. 'Le scepticisme de Hume', *Revue phil.* 115,
61–127 (and 117 [1934], 161–225)
PEARDON, T. P. *The Transition in English Historical Writing,
1760–1830*, esp. 19–23. New York & London.
SCHAZMANN, P.-E. *La Comtesse de Boufflers*, ch. 5
('Un philosophe anglais à Paris'). Lausanne.

[**1934**]

ANDERSON, W. *An orientation of Hume's moral philosophy.*
Chicago (diss.).
DE MICHELIS, E. 'Il problema e il metodo della critica
gnoseologica secondo David Hume', *Riv. Fil.* 25, 219–44.
EVANS, M. P. *The conception of the self in Locke, Berkeley and
Hume.* U. of Wales (diss.).
HOLMBERG, O. 'David Hume in Carlyle's *Sartor Resartus*',
Årsberättelse, Kungl. humanistika Vetenskapssamfundet i Lund,
91–109.
HOLT, E. B. 'The argument for sensationism as drawn from
Dr. Berkeley', *Psychol. Rev.* 41, 509–33.
LAIRD, J. *Hobbes*, chs. 8–9. London. (repr. 1968, New York)
LAIRD, J. 'Opinions récentes sur Hume', *Rech. phil.* 3, 363–81.
PFEIL, H. *Der Psychologismus im englischen Empirismus*,
101–80. Paderborn.

SMITH, Preserved. *A History of Modern Culture*, vol. 2,
esp. ch. 5, sec. 5. New York. (repr. 1962 as *The Enlightenment, 1687–1776*, New York)

[1935]

ABBOTT, W. C. *Adventures in Reputation*, 118–46
('David Hume: Philosopher-Historian'). Cambridge, Mass.
ANDERSON, J. 'Design', *Australas. J. Phil.* 13, 241–56.
(repr. 1962 in his *Studies in Empirical Philosophy*, Sydney)
CARRITT, E. F. *Morals and Politics*, ch. 5 (47–55). Oxford.
CHURCH, R. W. *Hume's Theory of the Understanding*. London.
(repr. 1968, Hamden, Conn.)
[*P* 10 (1935) 370–3; *JP* 32 (1935) 691; *M* 45 (1936) 536–7;
PR 46 (1937) 89–91]
DAL VERME, M. E. 'Osservazioni sul concetto di esistenza in
Hume', *Riv. Fil. neo-scolastica* 27, 87–91.
KEMP SMITH, N. *Hume's Dialogues Concerning Natural
Religion*. Oxford. (2nd edn London 1947; repr. 1962,
New York)
[*TLS* (2 Nov. 1935) 686; *JP* 32 (1935) 665–6;
M 45 (1936) 334–49; *PR* 45 (1936) 619–20;
P 11 (1936) 208–9; *JTS* 37 (1936) 337–49;
P 12 (1937) 175–90; *P* 13 (1938) 84–6]
MAGNINO, B. *Il pensiero filosofico di David Hume*. Naples.
MAUND, C. 'Hume's Treatment of Simples', *Proc. Arist. Soc.*
35, 209–28. (cf. Maund 1937, chs. 3–4)
PEIRCE, C. S. 'Hume on Miracles' [c. 1901], in C. Hartshorne
& P. Weiss, *Collected Papers of Charles Sanders Peirce*, vol. 6,
356–69. Cambridge, Mass. (repr. 1960)
SCIACCA, M. F. 'Due saggi letterari di David Hume', in *Studi
sulla filosofia medioevale e moderna*, 125–35. Naples.
STANLEY, P. 'The Scepticisms of David Hume', *J. Phil.* 32,
421–31.
WELCH, L. *Imagination and Human Nature*, 69–73. London.
WHEELWRIGHT, P. *Hume, A Treatise of Human Nature,
Book 1*. New York. [*JP* 32 (1935) 613]

[1936]

BAYLEY, F. C. *The Causes and Evidence of Beliefs: An
examination of Hume's procedure*. (Columbia U., diss.).
Mount Hermon, Mass. [*JCA* 4 (1973) 141–53]

BOYS SMITH, J. S. 'Hume's *Dialogues Concerning Natural Religion*', *J. theol. Studies* 37, 337–49.

EBERT, H. F. *Jean-Jacques Rousseau und David Hume*. Würzburg (diss.).

GOUGH, J. W. *The Social Contract*, ch. 12. Oxford. (2nd edn 1957)

HERTZ, P. 'Kritische Bemerkungen zu Reichenbachs Behandlung des Humeschen Problems', *Erkenntnis* 6, 25–31.

MEINECKE, F. *Die Entstehung des Historismus*, ch. 5 ('Die englische Aufklärungshistorie'), sec. 1 ('Hume').
Munich & Berlin. (repr. 1959 as vol. 3 of his *Werke*, Munich) (transl. 1972 as *Historism*, London)

MOSSNER, E. C. 'The Enigma of Hume', *Mind* 45, 334–49.

SCHEFFER, J. D. 'The Idea of Decline in Literature and the Fine Arts in Eighteenth-Century England', *Mod. Philol.* 34, 155–78.

TAUBE, M. *Causation, Freedom and Determinism*, ch. 4. London.

[**1937**]

BONIVENTO, O. *Alcune considerazioni sui rapporti dei fondamenti della morale di D. Hume e di E. Kant.* (47 pp.) Bologna.

CANDELORO, G. 'Il pensiero politico di David Hume', *G. critico Fil. ital.* 18, 335–55 and 408–24.

DAL VERME, M. E. 'Intorno all'influenza esercitata da Cartesio su Hume a proposito del problema dell'anima umana e della sua unione col corpo', *Cartesio nel terzo centenario del 'Discorso'*, suppl. to *Riv. Fil. neo-scolastica* 29, 239–47.

DAVIES, O. R. *The theory of universals, with special reference to Locke, Berkeley and Hume*. U. of Wales (diss.).

DOERING, J. F. 'Hume and the Theory of Tragedy', *PMLA* 52, 1130–4.

DOI, Torakazu. *Hume*. Kyoto.

FABRO, C. L'origine psicologica della nozione di causa', *Riv. Fil. neo-scolastica* 29, 207–44.

GIORGIANTONIO, M. 'Hume e Descartes', *Sophia* 5, 30–40.

HEDENIUS, I. 'Studies in Hume's Ethics', in Hedenius et al., *Adolf Phalén in Memoriam: Philosophical Essays*, 388–485. Uppsala & Stockholm.
[*P* 13 (1938) 498–9; *JP* 35 (1938) 440–3]

JOHNSON, E. A. J. *Predecessors of Adam Smith: The Growth of British Economic Thought*, ch. 9. New York. (repr. 1960, New York).

LAING, B. M. 'Hume's *Dialogues concerning Natural Religion*', *Philosophy* 12, 175–90. [*P* 13 (1938) 84–6]

LAING, B. M. 'Great Thinkers: (XII) David Hume', *Philosophy* 12, 395–412.

LEROY, A.-L. 'Les procédés du bon sens et la méthode de la science de l'homme pour David Hume', in *Travaux du IXᵉ Congrès int. Phil . . . Descartes*, vol. 5, 154–60. Paris.

MARHENKE, P. 'Hume's View of Identity', in *The Problem of the Individual* (U. of Calif. Publications in Philosophy, 20), 157–80. Berkeley, Cal. (repr. 1969, New York)

MARTEGANI, G. 'Studi sul Cartesio e sullo Hume', *Civiltà Cattolica* 88, no. 3, 53–60.

MAUND, C. *Hume's Theory of Knowledge: A critical examination*. London. (repr. 1972, New York)
[*P* 12 (1937) 488–9; *M* 47 (1938) 104–6; *JP* 35 (1938) 475; *Scholastik* 14 (1939) 437–8]

PIAGET, J. *La construction du réel chez l'enfant*, ch. 3, sec. 6. Neuchâtel & Paris. (transl. 1954 as *The Child's Construction of Reality*)

SABINE, G. H. *A History of Political Theory*, ch. 29. New York. (2nd edn 1951; 3rd edn 1961; 4th edn 1973)

SEGERSTEDT, T. T. *Moral Sense-skolan och dess inflytande på svensk filosofi*. Lund. [*JP* 35 (1938) 498]

[1938]

BROWN, S. G. 'Observations on Hume's Theory of Taste', *Engl. Studies* 20, 193–8.

CHURCH, R. W. 'Malebranche and Hume', *Revue int. Phil.* 1, 143–61.

COLLINGWOOD, R. G. *The Principles of Art*, chs. 9–10. Oxford.

DAL VERME, M. E. 'Di alcuni rapporti fra Malebranche e Hume', in *Malebranche*, suppl. to *Riv. Fil. neo-scolastica* 30, 303–11.

GUI, L. 'Lo scetticismo e la sua soluzione scettica nel pensiero di David Hume', *Riv. Fil. neo-scolastica* 30, 14–43 and 534–9.

JESSOP, T. E. *A Bibliography of David Hume and of Scottish Philosophy, from Francis Hutcheson to Lord Balfour*. London & Hull. (repr. 1966, New York)
[*P* 14 (1939) 236; *Revue Sci. phil. & théol.* 29 (1940) 118; *New Scholasticism* 42 (1968) 335–6]

JOAD, C. E. M. *Guide to the Philosophy of Morals and Politics*, ch. 10, sec. 2 (361–7: 'Subjectivist-Utilitarian Ethics'). London.

KAILA, E. 'David Humen Kolme Kausaaliprobleemaa',
Ajatus 9, 188–209.
KARITZ, A. *Till tolkningen av Berkeley och Hume.* (88 pp.)
Uppsala.
KEYNES, J. M. & SRAFFA, P. *An Abstract of a Treatise of
Human Nature* (1740): *a Pamphlet Hitherto Unknown,
by David Hume.* Cambridge. (repr. 1965, Hamden, Conn.)
[*M* 47 (1938) 520–2; *JP* 35 (1938) 639–40; *RMM* 45,
suppl. (1938) 1–2; *Int. J. Ethics* 49 (1938) 123; *P* 14 (1939)
116–17; *PR* 48 (1939) 643–4; *GCFI* 20 (1939) 487–8]
MACLAGAN, W. G. 'Letters of David Hume', let. to *TLS*
(1 Oct.), 627.
MOSSNER, E. C. 'Hume's *Dialogues Concerning Natural
Religion*: An Answer to Dr. Laing', *Philosophy* 13, 84–6.
(on Laing 1937)
REICHENBACH, H. *Experience and Prediction*, secs. 38–40.
Chicago.
RODDIER, H. 'La Querelle Rousseau-Hume', *Revue Litt. comp.*
18, 452–77.
ROLL, E. *A History of Economic Thought*, ch. 3. London.
(2nd edn 1945; 3rd edn 1954)
RUTRLE, O. 'Úvaha nad Masarykovou kapitolou o Kantově
překonání Humeovy skepsy v knize "Moderní člověk a
náboženství"', *Náboženská revue* 3, 135–40.
RYAN, J. K. 'Aquinas and Hume on the Laws of Association',
New Scholasticism 12, 366–77.
WALLENFELS, W. *Die Rechtsphilosophie David Humes.*
Göttingen (diss.).
WATERS, B. 'Positivistic and Activistic Theories of Causation',
J. Phil. 35, 85–93.
ZIEGELMEYER, E. H. *The relation between empiricism and
scepticism in Hume's theory of knowledge.* London, King's Coll.
(diss.).

[**1939**]

ALDRICH, V. C. 'Two Hundred Years after Hume's *Treatise*',
J. Phil. 36, 600–5.
BEAULAVON, G. 'Un opuscule retrouvé de David Hume',
Revue Mét. 46, 375–97. (review and transl. of the *Abstract*)
BEAULAVON, G. 'Les derniers moments de David Hume
d'après les papiers intimes de Boswell', *Revue Mét.* 46,
471–6. (transl. of Boswell's report)

BERGER, G. 'Husserl et Hume', *Revue int. Phil.* 1, 342–53. (repr. 1964 in his *Phénoménologie du temps et Prospective*, Paris; also 1973 in German transl. in H. Noack, *Husserl*, Darmstadt)

DELLA VOLPE, G. 'Il problema dell'esistenza in Aristotele, Hume e Kant, e il suo rapporto con quello estetico', *Annali Fac. Mag. r. Univ. Messina*. Palermo.

DELLA VOLPE, G. *Hume o il genio dell'empirismo*. (2nd edn of Della Volpe 1933) Florence.
[*RMM* 47 (1940) 258; *PR* 50 (1941) 247; *Les Sci. phil. & théol.* 2 (1941–2) 478]

DOERING, J. F. 'David Hume on Oratory', *Q.J. Speech* 25, 409–16.

FLORIAN, M. *Cunoaştere şi existenţă*, 99–123 ('Filosofia lui Hume ca impas al cugetării occidentale'). Bucharest.

HEINEMANN, F. H. 'Letters of Hume', let. to *TLS* (28 Jan.), 58. (on Klibansky below)

HOERNLÉ, R. F. A. 'A Misprint in Certain Editions of Hume's *Enquiry concerning . . . Morals*', *Mind* 48, 270.

KEMP SMITH, N. 'David Hume, 1739–1939', *Proc. Arist. Soc.* suppl. vol. 18, pp. i–xxxiv. (mostly repr. 1941, with some additions, as ch. 24 and also pp. 243–6 and 285–9 of his *The Philosophy of David Hume*)

KLIBANSKY, R. 'Letters of Hume', let. to *TLS* (21 Jan.), 41. (on Maclagan 1938)

KRUSE, V. *Hume's Philosophy in his Principal Work*, '*A Treatise of Human Nature*' *and in his Essays*. Transl. by P. E. Federspiel. London.
[*M* 49 (1940) 87–94; *P* 15 (1940) 106; *Tidsskrift for Rettsvitenskap* 54 (1941) 425–34 and 55 (1942) 77–81]

LAIRD, J. 'Hume's Account of Sensitive Belief', *Mind* 48, 427–45.

MAIDMENT, H. J. 'In Defence of Hume on Miracles', *Philosophy* 14, 422–33.

METZ, R. 'Eine neuentdeckte Schrift Humes. Zur Erinnerung an die 200. Wiederkehr des Erscheinungsjahres des *Treatise of Human Nature*', *Blätter für deutsche Philosophie* 12, 405–15.

RODDIER, H. 'A propos de la querelle Rousseau-Hume: précisions chronologiques', *Revue d'histoire littéraire de la France* 46, 211–14.

ROMERO, F. *Hume y el problema de la causalidad*. (13 pp.) Buenos Aires.

TAYLOR, A. E.; LAIRD, J.; and JESSOP, T. E. 'The Present-
Day Relevance of Hume's *Dialogues concerning Natural
Religion*', *Proc. Arist. Soc.* suppl. vol. 18, 179–228.

TREE, R. J. *The relation of theology to epistemology, with special
reference to Hume.* U. of Wales (diss.).

[**1940**]

AYER, A. J. *The Foundations of Empirical Knowledge*, sec. 18
('The Animistic Idea of Necessary Connexion'). London.

EVANS, F. B. 'Shelley, Godwin, Hume and the Doctrine of
Necessity', *Studies in Philol.* 15, 632–40.

GURWITSCH, A. 'On the Intentionality of Consciousness'
[sec. on 'The Problem of Identity as Stated by Hume'], in
M. Farber, *Philosophical Essays in Memory of Edmund Husserl.*
Cambridge, Mass. (repr. 1966 in Gurwitsch, *Studies in
Phenomenology and Psychology*, Evanston, Ill.)

HEINEMANN, F. H. *David Hume: The Man and His Science of
Man, Containing Some Unpublished Letters of Hume.* (65 pp.)
Paris.
[*P* 16 (1941) 326–7; let. to *TLS* (15 Mar. 1942) 127;
PR 51 (1942) 423–5]

JOHNSTON, J. 'Locke, Berkeley and Hume as Monetary
Theorists', *Hermathena* no. 56, 77–83.

MOSSNER, E. C. 'Hume and the Scottish Shakespeare',
Huntington Lib. Q. 3, 419–41. (repr. 1943, in revised and
expanded form, as ch. 3 of his *The Forgotten Hume*)

OAKE, R. B. 'Did Maupertius read Hume's *Treatise of Human
Nature*?', *Revue Litt. comp.* 20, 81–7.

PRICE, H. H. *Hume's Theory of the External World.* Oxford.
[*M* 50 (1941) 156; *JP* 38 (1941) 609–13; *P* 16 (1941)
316–18]

PRICE, H. H. 'The Permanent Significance of Hume's
Philosophy', *Philosophy* 15, 7–37. (repr. 1965 in
Sesonske & Fleming, *Human Understanding*)

VÁZQUEZ, J. A. 'Una obra de Hume casi desconocida
(1740–1940)', *Nosotros* (Buenos Aires) 5, 404–11.

WILLEY, B. *The Eighteenth Century Background*, ch. 7
(110–35: 'David Hume, Defender of "Nature" against
"Reason"'). London.

CHURCH, R. W. 'Hume's Theory of Philosophical Relations',
   Phil. Rev. 50, 353–67.

DINGLE, R. J. 'The Scepticism of David Hume', *Nineteenth
   Century* 129, 570–4.

GARIN, E. *L'illuminismo inglese: i moralisti.* Milan.

GROSS, M. W. 'Whitehead's Answer to Hume: A Reply',
   J. Phil. 38, 95–102. (on Robson below) (repr. 1963 in
   G. L. Kline, *Alfred North Whitehead: Essays on his philosophy*,
   Englewood Cliffs, N.J.)

HEDENIUS, I. 'David Hume', *Studiekamraten* 43, 118–19.
   (repr. 1949 as 'De båda versionerna av Humes filosofi',
   in *Tro och vetande*, 319–30, Stockholm)

HEINEMANN, F. H. 'Hume as Philosopher', let. to *TLS*
   (12 April), 179.

KEMP SMITH, N. *The Philosophy of David Hume: A critical
   study of its origins and central doctrines.* London. (chs. 4–6
   contain his articles from *Mind* 1905 almost verbatim)
   [*HJ* 39 (1940–1) 436–8; *TLS* (1 March 1941) 102;
   M 51 (1942) 69–75; *JTS* 43 (1942) 229–32; *NS* 17 (1943)
   182–4; *P* 23 (1948) 264–8; *RP* 73 (1948) 235–41;
   Sth. J. Phil. 7 (1969) 3–7]

MOSSNER, E. C. 'Was Hume a Tory Historian? Facts and
   Reconsiderations', *J. Hist. Ideas* 2, 225–36.
   [*Philol. Q.* 21 (1942) 206–9]

MOSSNER, E. C. 'An Apology for David Hume, Historian',
   PMLA 56, 657–90. [*Philol. Q.* 21 (1942) 206–9]

OAKE, R. B. 'Montesquieu and Hume', *Mod. Lang. Q.* 2,
   25–41 and 225–48. [*Philol. Q.* 21 (1942) 209–10]

ROBSON, J. W. 'Whitehead's Answer to Hume', *J. Phil.* 38,
   85–95. [95–102] (both repr. 1963 in G. L. Kline, *Alfred
   North Whitehead: Essays on his philosophy*,
   Englewood Cliffs, N.J.)

SUTER, R. 'A Skeptic among the Scientists', *Scientific Monthly*
   53, 565–8.

TAYLOR, H. 'Hume's Answer to Whitehead', *J. Phil.* 38, 409–16.

TREE, R. J. *An examination of Hume's treatment of the problems
   of divine existence and providence.* Oxford U. (diss.).

VON WRIGHT, G. H. *The Logical Problem of Induction*, ch. 2.
   Helsingfors. (2nd edn Oxford 1957)

WOOZLEY, A. D. *Thomas Reid, Essays on the Intellectual
   Powers of Man*, introduction. London.

AARON, R.I. 'Hume's Theory of Universals', *Proc. Arist.
Soc.* 42, 117–40.

BALDENSPERGER, F. 'La première relation intellectuelle de
David Hume en France: une conjecture', *Mod. Lang. Notes* 57,
268–71.

CHURCH, R.W. *Bradley's Dialectic*, 172–81. London.

GUILLEMIN, H. '*Cette affaire infernale': l'affaire
J.-J. Rousseau–David Hume*, 1766. (356 pp.) Paris.
[*Étud. class.* 11 (1942) 408–9; *Revue Hist. Phil.* (1944) 85–6;
Romanic Rev. 39 (1948) 75–8]

LEÓN BURGEOIS, E. 'La filosofía especulativa de David Hume',
Estudios (Chile), 111, 22–47.

MARCHETTI, G. 'Lo sviluppo della problematica nominalistica
nell'empirismo inglese da Locke a Hume', in *Saggi*.
Porto Empedocle.

MOSSNER, E.C. 'Hume as Literary Patron: A Suppressed
Review of Robert Henry's *History of Great Britain*, 1773',
Mod. Philol. 39, 361–82. (Hume's text itself is repr. 1965 in
Norton & Popkin, *David Hume: Philosophical Historian*,
377–88)

ROSS, W.G. *Human Nature and Utility in Hume's Social
Philosophy.* (xiii, 107 pp.) New York. (repr. 1976, New York)

WALLIS, W.D. 'David Hume's Contribution to Social Science',
in F.P. Clarke & M.C. Nahm, *Philosophical Essays in honor of
Edgar Arthur Singer, Jr.*, 358–71. Philadelphia.

AIKEN, H.D. *The moral philosophy of David Hume.*
Harvard U. (diss.).

BARATONO, A. *Hume e l'illuminismo inglese.* Milan. (anthol.)

BEARDSLEY, M.C. 'A Dilemma for Hume' [about causation],
Phil. Rev. 52, 28–46.

GRENE, M. 'Hume: Sceptic and Tory?', *J. Hist. Ideas* 4,
333–48.

GURWITSCH, A. 'William James's Theory ...' [section on
'Hume's Account of Temporality'], *Phil. & phenomenol. Res.* 3,
452–7. (repr. 1966 in Gurwitsch, *Studies in Phenomenology
and Psychology*, Evanston, Ill.)

LAIRD, J. 'Impressions and Ideas: A Note on Hume', *Mind* 52,
171–7.

METZ, R. 'Englandhass, Frankophilie und Deutschlandbild
bei David Hume', *Neuphilologische Monatsschrift* 14, 8–19.

MOSSNER, E. C. *The Forgotten Hume: Le bon David.* New York.
(repr. 1967)
[*Mod. Philol.* 41 (1943) 123–6; *JP* 40 (1943) 278–9;
PR 52 (1943) 610–11; *Philol. Q.* 23 (1944) 167–9;
MLR 39 (1944) 197–8]
SARNO, F. 'Nota sullo Hume', in *Pensiero e poesia.* Bari.
SMITH, A. H. *A Treatise on Knowledge*, ch. 1 (1–58). Oxford.
TAYLOR, H. 'Hume's Theory of Imagination', *U. Toronto Q.* 12,
180–90.

[1944]

CLOUGH, W. O. 'Reason and Genius—An Eighteenth-Century
Dilemma', *Philol. Q.* 23, 33–54.
MOSSNER, E. C. 'Hume's Epistle to Dr. Arbuthnot, 1734:
The Biographical Significance', *Huntington Libr. Q.* 7, 135–52.
STEVENSON, C. L. *Ethics and Language*, ch. 12, sec. 5.
New Haven.

[1945]

BRYSON, G. *Man and Society: The Scottish inquiry of the
eighteenth century*, esp. 102–9, 198–205, and 225–35.
Princeton. (repr. 1968, New York)
[*Philol. Q.* 25 (1946) 136–42]
HEIMANN, E. *History of Economic Doctrines*, ch. 2. New York.
MILLER, D. S. 'An Event in Modern Philosophy', *Phil. Rev.* 54,
593–606. (repr. 1975 in Miller, *Philosophical Analysis and
Human Welfare*, Dordrecht & Boston)

[1946]

COLLINGWOOD, R. G. *The Idea of History*, pt. 2, secs. 8–10.
Oxford.
KALLICH, M. 'The Associationist Criticism of Francis
Hutcheson and David Hume', *Studies in Philology* 43,
644–67. (repr. in Kallich 1970)
KYDD, R. M. *Reason and Conduct in Hume's Treatise.* (Oxford
classical & philosophical monographs) London. (repr. 1964,
New York)
[*M* 55 (1946) 273–4; *HJ* 44 (1946) 382–4;
P 22 (1947) 92–3; *JP* 46 (1949) 796–7]
LEROY, A. *David Hume, Traité de la nature humaine.* 2 vols.
Paris.

MARIE-DE-LOURDES, R. J.-M. 'Essai de commentaire
critique sur l' *Enquiry Concerning Human Understanding* de
David Hume', *Laval théologique et philosophique* 2, 9–56 and
3, 58–78.

MAXWELL, J. C. 'An Allusion in Hume's *Letters*', *Notes &
Queries* 190, 228–30.

MAXWELL, J. C. 'Hume's Treatment of Identity', *Australas. J.
Phil.* 24, 183–7.

MICHOTTE, A. *La Perception de la Causalité*, ch. 17. Louvain.
(2nd edn 1954) (transl. 1963 by T. R. & E. Miles as *The
Perception of Causality*, London; with Commentary by
T. R. Miles, of which pp. 410–15 are on Hume)
[Macnabb 1974]

PRICE, K. B. *Metaphysics in relation to ethics: a study of Hume*.
U. of Calif., Berkeley (diss.).

RUSSELL, B. *History of Western Philosophy*, bk. 3, ch. 17.
London.

[1947]

AIKEN, H. D. 'The Moral Philosophy of David Hume',
Harvard U. Grad. Sch. . . . summaries of theses . . ., 546–51.
Cambridge, Mass. (cf. Aiken 1943).

BAGOLINI, L. *Esperienza giuridica e politica nel pensiero di
David Hume*. Siena. (2nd edn Turin 1967)
[*M* 57 (1948) 366–73; *E* 59 (1949) 304; *PR* 59 (1950) 564–6]

BROWNING, R. W. *Reason in ethics and morals, with special
reference to . . . Hume and Dewey*. U. of Calif., Berkeley (diss.).

BURTT, E. A. 'Value and Existence', *J. Phil.* 44, 169–79.

COURTINES, P. 'Bayle, Hume and Berkeley', *Revue Litt. comp.*
21, 416–28.

DUNHAM, J. H. *The Religion of Philosophers*, ch. 9.
(Temple U. Publications) Philadelphia.

LEES-MILNE, J. *The Age of Adam*, 14–17. London.

LEWIS, C. S. *Miracles: A preliminary study*, ch. 13. London.
[Flew 1961, 192–3].

MILLER, D. S. 'Professor Donald Williams versus Hume',
J. Phil. 44, 673–84. (repr. 1966 in M. H. Foster &
M. L. Martin, *Probability, Confirmation, and Simplicity*,
New York)

MOSSNER, E. C. 'The Continental Reception of Hume's
Treatise, 1739–1741', *Mind* 56, 31–43.

MOSSNER, E.C. 'David Hume's "An Historical Essay on
Chivalry and modern Honour"', *Mod. Philol.* 45, 54–60.

[1947 contd.] 43

RANDALL, J.H., Jr. 'David Hume: Radical Empiricist and
Pragmatist', in S.Hook & M.R.Konvitz, *Freedom and
Experience*, 289–312. Ithaca, N.Y. (repr. 1962 as ch. 5 of
bk. 4 of Randall, *The Career of Philosophy, From the Middle
Ages to the Enlightenment*, New York & London)

RAPHAEL, D.D. *The Moral Sense*, ch. 3. (Oxford classical &
philosophical monographs) London.

SCHACK, T. 'David Humes Kritik af Religionen', in Schack,
Afhandlinger, 208–31. Copenhagen.

SHIMONY, A. 'An Ontological Examination of Causation',
Rev. Met. 1, 52–68.

WALSH, W.H. *Reason and Experience*, 176–85. Oxford.

WIENER, P.P. 'Letters [by C.S. Peirce] to Samuel P.Langley,
and "Hume on Miracles and Laws of Nature"', *Proc. Am.
phil. Soc.* 91, 201–228. (repr. 1958 in Wiener, *Values in a
Universe of Chance*, Stanford, Calif.; & New York. This was
itself repr. 1966 as Charles S. Peirce, *Selected Writings*,
New York)

WILL, F.L. 'Will the Future Be Like the Past?' *Mind* 56,
332–47. (repr. 1953 in A.Flew, *Logic and Language*, Second
Series, Oxford; 1957 in P.Edwards & A.Pap, *A Modern
Introd. to Philosophy*, Glencoe, Ill.; and in Mandelbaum
et al., *Philosophic Problems*)

WOLFSON, H.A. 'Causality and Freedom in Descartes, Leibniz,
and Hume', in Hook & Konvitz, op. cit., [see Randall above]
97–114.

[**1948**]

ABBAGNANO, N. *Storia della filosofia*, vol. 2, ch. 10. Turin.

AIKEN, H.D. *Hume's Dialogues concerning Natural Religion*.
(Hafner Library of Classics, 5) New York.

AIKEN, H.D. *Hume's Moral and Political Philosophy*. (Hafner
Library of Classics, 3) New York. (anthol.)
[*PR* 57 (1948) 429]

BANDY, W.T. 'A Sidelight on the Hume-Rousseau Quarrel',
Mod. Lang. Notes 63, 486.

BANDY, W.T. 'Rousseau's flight from England', *Romanic
Rev.* 39, 107–21.

BIANCA, G. *La credenza come fondamento dell'attività pratica
in Locke e in Hume.* (230 pp.) Catania. (2nd edn Padua 1950)
[*Sapienza* 3 (1950), 109–11]

BRICE, J.I. *The influence of Hume in British theology.* London,
Richmond Coll. (diss.).

FRIEDRICH, C. J. *Inevitable Peace*, 149–57 and 188–95. Cambridge, Mass.

GRAFFEO, A. 'La filosofia humiana del diritto', *Atti dell' Accad. di Scienze, Lettere e Arti di Palermo*.

KARLIN, E. 'The Nature of Causation', *Rev. Met.* 2, 53–98.

MOSSNER, E. C. 'Beattie's "The Castle of Scepticism": An Unpublished Allegory against Hume, Voltaire, and Hobbes', (*U. of Texas*) *Studies in English* 27, 108–45.

MOSSNER, E. C. 'Hume's Early *Memoranda*, 1729–1740: The Complete Text', *J. Hist. Ideas* 9, 492–518.

MOSSNER, E. C. 'Dr. Johnson *in partibus Infidelium* ?', *Mod. Lang. Notes* 63, 516–19.

NAESS, A. *Noen verditeoretiske standpunkter* (Some Axiological Points of View). Oslo. (mimeo.)

RUTSKI, J. *Doktryna Hume'a o prawdopodobieństwie. Uwagi w sprawie jej interpretacji*. (55 pp.) Toruń.

[**1949**]

ALDRIDGE, A. O. 'Polygamy and Deism', *J. Engl. & Germanic Philol.* 48, 343–60. (pp. 356–7 are on Hume's essay 'Of Polygamy and Divorces')

CAIRNS, H. *Legal Philosophy from Plato to Hegel*, ch. 11. Baltimore.

CARRÉ, M. H. *Phases of Thought in England*, 297–301. Oxford.

CONTE, A. 'Une philosophie sans nom', *Actas prim. Congreso nacion. Fil. Argentin.* 3, 1931–7.

DAL PRA, M. *Hume.* (*Storia universale della Filosofia*, vol. 16) Milan. (rev. edn 1973, Rome & Bari) [*RP* 143 (1952) 275]

DAL PRA, M. 'Malebranche nell'opera di Hume', *Riv. crit. Stor. Fil.* 4, 297–9.

ELLIOTT, R. C. 'Hume's "Character of Sir Robert Walpole": Some Unnoticed Additions', *J. Engl. & Germanic Philol.* 48, 367–70.

HÖLLHUBER, I. 'Sullo pseudo-idealismo del Locke, del Berkeley e dello Hume', *Humanitas* 4, 150–6.

KING, H. R. 'From St. Thomas, Ockham, and the intelligible species, to Thomism, Hume, and the sensible species', *Dominican Studies* 2, 93–103.

KING, H. R. 'Whitehead's Doctrine of Causal Efficacy', *J. Phil.* 46, 85–100.

KNEALE, W. *Probability and Induction*, secs. 13–18. Oxford.

LEROY, A.-L. 'La liberté de spontanéité chez David Hume', in *La Liberté: Actes du IVe Congrès des Sociétés de Philosophie de Langue Française*, 363–7. Neuchâtel.

LEROY, A.-L. 'L'idée de la nature humaine d'après David Hume', *Proc. Xth int. Congr. Phil.*, vol. 2, 1160–2. Amsterdam.

LODGE, R. C. *The Great Thinkers*, ch. 9. London.

MACLAGAN, W. G. 'Hume's Attitude to Religion', *Proc. R. phil. Soc. Glasgow* 74, 83. (abstract of lecture)

MILLER, D. S. 'Hume's Deathblow to Deductivism', *J. Phil.* 46, 745–62. (repr. 1975 in Miller, *Philosophical Analysis and Human Welfare*, Dordrecht & Boston)

MOSSNER, E. C. 'Hume and the Ancient-Modern Controversy, 1725–1752: A Study in Creative Scepticism', (*U. of Texas*) *Studies in English* 28, 139–53.

MOSSNER, E. C. 'A MS. Fragment of Hume's *Treatise*, 1740', *Notes & Queries* 194, 520–2. (a description; for full publication, see Nidditch 1976, pp. 50–5)

PARESCE, E. 'Hume, Hamann, Kierkegaard e la filosofia della credenza', *Riv. int. Fil. Diritto* 26, 357–75.

PLAMENATZ, J. *The English Utilitarians*, ch. 2. Oxford. (2nd edn 1958)

PRIOR, A. N. *Logic and the Basis of Ethics*, passim. Oxford. [*M* 59 (1950) 392–5; *JP* 48 (1951) 310–11]

REICHENBACH, H. *The Theory of Probability*, sec. 91. Berkeley & Los Angeles. (repr. 1966 in M. H. Foster & M. L. Martin, *Probability, Confirmation, and Simplicity*, New York)

REICHENBACH, H. 'A Conversation between Bertrand Russell and David Hume', *J. Phil.* 46, 545–9.

RUDDICK, C. T. 'Hume on Scientific Law', *Phil. Sci.* 16, 89–93.

STACE, W. T. 'The Parmenidean Dogma', *Philosophy* 24, 195–204.

STERNFELD, R. 'The Unity of Hume's *Enquiry Concerning Human Understanding*', *Rev. Met.* 3, 167–88.

WILD, J. 'A Realistic Defence of Causal Efficacy', *Rev. Met.* 3, 1–14.

YALDEN-THOMSON, D. C. *Hume's moral philosophy in the 'Treatise...'*. McGill U. (diss.).

[1950]

BARTOLASO, G. 'Il concetto di causa da Hume agli scienziati moderni', *Civiltà Cattolica* 101, no. 3, 17–25.

DE RUVO, V. *Il problema della verità da Spinoza a Hume*. (viii, 296 pp.) Padua.

GLATHE, A.B. *Hume's Theory of the Passions and of Morals: A Study of Books II and III of the 'Treatise'*. (U. of Calif. Publications in Phil., 24) Berkeley. (repr. 1969, New York)

HARTNACK, J. *Analysis of the Problem of Perception in British Empiricism*, ch. 3 (104–46). Copenhagen.

HERUDAY, J.C. *David Hume's Theory of Human Assent*. Rome.

JONAS, H. 'Causality and Perception', *J. Phil.* 47, 319–24.

LAIRD, J. 'Hume, David', in *Chambers's Encyclopaedia* (new edition). London.

LAZEROWITZ, M. 'Substratum', in Max Black, *Philosophical Analysis*, 176–94. Ithaca, N.Y. (repr. 1963, Englewood Cliffs, N.J. The article was also repr. 1955 in Lazerowitz, *The Structure of Metaphysics*, London)

LEROY, A.L. 'Des ambiguités de la philosophie de Hume', *Information philosophique* 1, 9–13.

McRAE, R. 'Final Causes in the Age of Reason', *U. Toronto Q.* 19, 247–58.

MOSSNER, E.C. 'Hume's *Four Dissertations*: An Essay in Biography and Bibliography', *Mod. Philol.* 48, 37–57.

MOSSNER, E.C. 'Philosophy and Biography: The case of David Hume', *Phil. Rev.* 59, 184–201. (repr. 1966 in Chappell, *Hume*)

MOSSNER, E.C. & RANSOM, H. 'Hume and the "Conspiracy of the Booksellers": The Publication and Early Fortunes of the *History of England*', (*U. of Texas*) *Studies in English* 29, 162–82.

NOYES, C.E. *Aesthetic theory and literary criticism in the works of David Hume*. U. of Texas (diss.).

PFLAUM, K.B. 'Hume's Treatment of Belief', *Australas. J. Phil.* 28, 93–113.

PRICE, K.B. 'Does Hume's Theory of Knowledge Determine his Ethical Theory?', *J. Phil.* 47, 425–34.

PRICE, K.B. 'Hume's Analysis of Generality', *Phil. Rev.* 59, 58–76.

PRICHARD, H.A. See 1932.

RODDIER, H.J.-J. *Rousseau en Angleterre au XVIIIᵉ siècle: L'oeuvre et l'homme*, ch. 7. Paris. [*Romanic Rev.* 42 (1951) 65–7]

SMART, H.R.G. *The theories of space and time found in Hume's writings*. Duke U. (diss.).

WARD SMITH, J. 'The British Moralists and the Fallacy of Psychologism', *J. Hist. Ideas* 11, 159–78.

WEINBERG, J. 'The Idea of Causal Efficacy', *J. Phil.* 47, 397–407.
WHITE, R. E. O. *Hume's theory of ethics: a study of the 'Enquiry . . .'.* U. of Liverpool (diss.).
WILL, F. L. 'Generalization and Evidence', in Max Black, *Philosophical Analysis*, 384–413. Ithaca, N.Y. (repr. 1963, Englewood Cliffs, N.J.)

[**1951**]

ATKINS, J. W. H. *English Literary Criticism: 17th and 18th Centuries*, 326–33. London.
BAGOLINI, L. 'A proposito di un saggio di Hume', *Riv. int. Fil. Diritto* 28, 427–30.
DUCASSE, C. J. *Nature, Mind and Death*, ch. 7. La Salle, Ill. (repr. 1960 in E. H. Madden, *The Structure of Scientific Thought*, 221–6, London. Also 1976 in M. Brand, *The Nature of Causation*, Urbana, Ill.)
GRADI, R. 'Razionalismo ed empirismo nel *Trattato* di David Hume', *Rass. Sci. fil.* 4, no. 2, 16–48, and no. 4, 23–32.
HAMILTON, C. S. *David Hume's contributions toward a theory of historical knowledge.* Yale U. (diss.).
KASTIL, A. *Die Philosophie Franz Brentanos*, 223–6. Salzburg.
LEROUX, E. & LEROY, A.-L. *La Philosophie anglaise classique*, ch. 8. Paris. [*Mind* 61 (1952) 122–6]
MACNABB, D. G. C. *David Hume: His Theory of Knowledge and Morality.* London. (2nd edn Oxford 1966)
[*TLS* (22 June 1951) 388; *P* 27 (1952) 270–1; *PQ* 2 (1952) 270–1; *M* 61 (1952) 126–7; *Month* 8 (Aug. 1952) 69–81]
McRAE, R. 'Hume as a Political Philosopher', *J. Hist. Ideas* 12, 285–90.
MAXWELL, J. C. 'Gibbon, Hume, and Julian the Apostate', *Notes & Queries* 196, 498.
MERLAN, P. 'From Hume to Hamann', *The Personalist* 32, 11–18. (repr. 1976 in his *Kleine Philosophische Schriften*, Hildesheim & New York)
MEYER, P. H. 'Voltaire and Hume's "Descent on the Coast of Brittany"', *Mod. Lang. Notes* 66, 429–35.
MOSSNER, E. C. 'The First Answer to Hume's *Treatise*: An Unnoticed Item of 1740', *J. Hist. Ideas* 12, 291–4.
OLIVER, W. D. *Theory of Order*, pt. 4 ('The Theory of Abstraction'), 258–71. Yellow Springs, Ohio.

POPKIN, R.H. 'David Hume: His Pyrrhonism and his Critique of Pyrrhonism', *Phil. Q.* 1, 385–407. (repr. 1966 in Chappell, *Hume* [*PQ* 3 (1953) 40–50]

POPKIN, R.H. 'Hume and Kierkegaard', *J. Relig.* 31, 274–81.

PRIOR, A.N. 'The Ethical Copula', *Australas. J. Phil.* 29, 137–54. (repr. 1976 in his *Papers in Logic and Ethics*, London)

REICHENBACH, H. *The Rise of Scientific Philosophy*, ch. 5 ('The Empiricist Approach'). Berkeley & Los Angeles.

SCHMITZ, R.M. 'In Deference to David Hume', *Washington U. Studies* 20, 1–13. (Hume's clerical friends at Edinburgh)

TODD, W.B. 'The First Printing of Hume's *Life* (1777)', *The Library* (ser. 5) 6, 123–5.

WASSERMAN, E.R. 'Unedited Letters by Sterne, Hume, and Rousseau', *Mod. Lang. Notes* 66, 73–80.

WATKINS, F. *Hume, Theory of Politics*. Edinburgh. (anthol.) [*PQ* 1 (1951) 461–2; *M* 61 (1952) 126; *P* 27 (1952) 268]

YALDEN-THOMSON, D.C. *Hume, Theory of Knowledge*. Edinburgh. (anthol.) [*PQ* 2 (1952) 270–1; *M* 61 (1952) 126–7; *PSt* (Irel.) 2 (1952) 119–21]

[1952]

AARON, R.I. *The Theory of Universals*, ch. 4. Oxford.

ACTON, H.B. 'Prejudice', *Revue int. Phil.* 6, 323–36.

AYER, A.J. & WINCH, R. *British Empirical Philosophers*. London. (anthol.) [*P* 28 (1953) 83–4]

BAGOLINI, L. *La simpatia nella morale e nel diritto*, ch. 5. Turin. (2nd edn 1966; 3rd edn 1975)

BOITEUX, L.-A. 'Le Rôle de d'Alembert dans la Querelle Rousseau-Hume', *Ann. Soc. J.-J. Rousseau* 33, 143–54.

BONGIE, L. L. *Hume en France au XVIIIᵉ siècle*. U. of Paris (diss.).

BONTADINI, G. *Indagini di struttura sul gnoseologismo moderno: Berkeley, Leibniz, Hume, Kant*, 87–144. Brescia.

BRENTANO, F. *Grundlegung und Aufbau der Ethik*, pt. 1, ch. 3. Berne. (transl. 1973 as *The Foundation and Construction of Ethics*, London & New York)

BRUNIUS, T. *David Hume on Criticism*. Stockholm. [*JP* 50 (1953) 20–2; *Philol. Q.* 32 (1953) 272–3; *PQ* 4 (1954) 275–6; *MLN* 69 (1954) 130–2; *RES* 5 (1954) 197–200; *Erasmus* 8 (1955) 648–9]

COHEN, R. *The critical theory of David Hume.* Columbia U. (diss.).

COPLESTON, F. 'David Hume and St John of the Cross', *The Month* 8, 69–81.

CRESSON, A. & DELEUZE, G. *David Hume: sa vie, son oeuvre, avec un exposé de sa philosophie.* Paris.
[*RP* 143 (1953) 273–4]

DAL PRA, M. 'Hume e Dewey', *Revue int. Phil.* 6, 236–49.

DAVIE, G. E. 'Hume and the Origins of the Common Sense School', *Revue int. Phil.* 6, 213–21.

FEN, S.-N. 'Has James Answered Hume ?', *J. Phil.* 49, 159–67.

JESSOP, T. E. 'Some Misunderstandings of Hume', *Revue int. Phil.* 6, 155–67. (repr. 1966 in Chappell, *Hume*)

LAFLEUR, L. J. 'A Footnote on Descartes and Hume', *J. Phil.* 49, 780–3. (on McLendon below)

LAMEERE, J. 'Notes bibliographiques', *Revue int. Phil.* 6, 250–3.

LEROY, A.-L. 'Statut de l'objet extérieur dans la philosophie de Hume', *Revue int. Phil.* 6, 199–212.

LEVETT, M. J. 'The Scepticism of David Hume', *Philosopher* 3, 62–71.

LOW, J. M. 'An Eighteenth Century Controversy in the Theory of Economic Progress', *Manchester Sch. Econ.* 20, 311–30.

McLENDON, H. J. 'Has Russell Answered Hume ?', *J. Phil.* 49, 145–59. [780–3]

MACNABB, D. G. C. 'Hume on Induction', *Revue int. Phil.* 6, 184–98.

MARKUS, R. I. 'Hume: Reason and Moral Sense', *Phil. & phenomenol. Res.* 13, 139–57.

MAUND, C. 'On the Nature and Significance of Hume's Scepticism', *Revue int. Phil.* 6, 168–83.

MEYER, P. H. 'The Manuscript of Hume's Account of His Dispute with Rousseau', *Comparative Lit.* 4, 341–50.

MOSSNER, E. C. 'Hume and the French Men of Letters', *Revue int. Phil.* 6, 222–35.

NISSEN, I. *Den Betingede Forpliktelse: En Studie over de pliktteorier som er fremsatt av David Hume og W. David Ross.* Oslo. [*PQ* 3 (1953) 84–5]

OLIVER, W. D. 'A Re-examination of the Problem of Induction', *J. Phil.* 49, 769–80.

PASSMORE, J. A. *Hume's Intentions.* Cambridge. (repr. 1968, London) [*M* 62 (1953) 568–70; *JP* 50 (1953) 472–80; *P* 29 (1954) 372–5; *PQ* 4 (1954) 89–90; *PR* 63 (1954) 113–16; *AJP* 32 (1954) 56–70; *E* 64 (1954) 315–16]

POPKIN, R. H. 'David Hume and the Pyrrhonian Controversy',
Rev. Met. 6, 65–81.

POPKIN, R. H. 'George Tucker, an Early American Critic of
Hume', *J. Hist. Ideas* 13, 370–5.

SHOUSE, J. B. 'David Hume and William James: A Comparison',
J. Hist. Ideas 13, 514–27.

STRINGA, M. L. 'Il problema di Hume: istinto e ragione',
Riv. Fil. 43, 420–39.

SUGG, R. S. *Hume and the British romantics.* U. of Texas (diss.).

[**1953**]

CORSI, M. *Natura e società in David Hume.* (xii, 80 pp.)
Florence. (anthol.)

DELEUZE, G. *Empirisme et subjectivité, Essai sur la Nature
humaine selon Hume.* Paris. (2nd edn Paris 1973)
[*RCSF* 9 (1954) 628–30]

DREVER, J. 'A Note on Hume's Pyrrhonism', *Phil. Q.* 3, 40–50.

FLEW, A. 'Images, Supposing, and Imagining', *Philosophy* 28,
246–54.

FRONDIZI, R. *The Nature of the Self*, ch. 4.
New Haven & London.

HALLIE, P. P. *Maine de Biran and the doctrines of Locke,
Berkeley and Hume.* Harvard U. (diss.).

HARRISON, J. 'Utilitarianism, Universalisation, and our duty
to be just', *Proc. Arist. Soc.* 53, 105–34. (repr. 1968 in
Bayles, *Contemporary Utilitarianism*; and in Thomson &
Dworkin, *Ethics*; also 1970 in Brody, *Moral Rules*)

HARTNACK, J. 'Some Remarks on Causality', *J. Phil.* 50,
466–71.

HENDEL, C. W. *David Hume's Political Essays.* New York.
[*JP* 52 (1955) 702–4]

LENZ, J. W. *Hume's skepticism and the experimental method of
reasoning.* Yale U. (diss.).

LEROY, A.-L. *David Hume.* (342 pp.) Paris.
[*PR* 63 (1954) 629–30; *PQ* 4 (1954) 275–6;
RFNS 46 (1954) 202–5; *JP* 52 (1955) 42–7;
M 64 (1955) 115–16]

MABBOTT, J. D. 'Reason and Desire', *Philosophy* 28, 113–23.
(repr. 1972 in R. F. Dearden et al., *Education and the
Development of Reason*, London)

MCCRACKEN, D. J. 'David Hume and the Sentiment of
Humanity', *Actes du XIe Congr. int. Phil.* vol. 13, 100–3.
Amsterdam & Louvain.

MOORE, G.E. *Some Main Problems of Philosophy*, chs. 5–6.
London. (On the limits of knowledge: cf. Moore, 'Hume's
Philosophy' *New Q*. 1909, repr. 1922 in his *Philosophical
Studies*, London)

POPKIN, R.H. 'The Sceptical Crisis and the Rise of Modern
Philosophy', *Rev. Met.* 7, 132–51 and 307–22, and 499–510
(1954).

POPKIN, R.H. 'Joseph Glanvill: A precursor of David Hume',
J. Hist. Ideas 14, 292–303.

PRICE, H.H. *Thinking and Experience*, 110–11, 134–40, and
284–6. (Sign-cognition and images) London.

RICCI, G. *Hume: acuto miope. Causalità: grimaldello della
ragione.* (21 pp.) Reggio Emilia.

STACE, W.T. *Religion and the Modern Mind*, ch. 8
('Naturalism'). London.

[**1954**]

BRUNET, O. 'David Hume: La Signification de sa Pensée',
Études anglaises 7, 294–301.

CARTER, W.B. *The status of universals in Locke, Berkeley and
Hume*. U. of Toronto (diss.).

GOLDMANN, E. 'Haroth lebiat ha indoxia', *Iyyun* 5, 286–96.

HARRIS, E.E. *Nature, Mind, and Modern Science*, ch. 8
('The Collapse of Empiricism'). London & New York.

HARTSHORNE, C. 'Causal Necessities: An Alternative to
Hume', *Phil. Rev.* 63, 479–99.

HATORI, T. 'Locke no Kokka-ron to England Jūshō-shugi—
Hume no Shosetsu tono Taihi' (Locke's theory of the state
and British mercantilism—a comparison with Hume's
theory), *Hitotsubashi Ronsō* 32, 259–93.

HOLLAND, R.F. 'The Empiricist Theory of Memory', *Mind* 63,
464–86. (repr. 1966 in Hampshire, *Philosophy of Mind*,
New York & London; 1971 in Levensky, *Human Factual
Knowledge*, Englewood Cliffs, N.J.)

KENNICK, W.E. *A methodological approach to metaphysics, with
special reference to Aristotle, Hume, Dewey and Whitehead.*
Cornell U. (diss.).

KLIBANSKY, R. & MOSSNER, E.C. *New Letters of David Hume.*
Oxford. (reissued 1970, Oxford)
[*P* 30 (1955) 375–6; *JP* 53 (1956) 203; *PQ* 6 (1956) 77–8;
Hist. Z. 182 (1956) 227–8; *M* 66 (1957) 266–8]

MARSHALL, G. 'David Hume and Political Scepticism',
Phil. Q. 4, 247–57.

MERLAN, P. 'Hamann et les *Dialogues* de Hume', *Revue Mét.* 59, 285–9. (repr. 1976 in his *Kleine Philosophische Schriften*, Hildesheim & New York)

MEYER, P. H. *Hume in eighteenth-century France*. Columbia U. (diss.).

MOSSNER, E. C. *The Life of David Hume*. Edinburgh. (repr. 1970, Oxford)
[*HJ* 53 (1955) 316–18; *Philol. Q.* 34 (1955) 296–8; *JP* 52 (1955) 802–10; *P* 31 (1956) 80–2; *Études anglaises* 9 (1956) 165–6; *M* 66 (1957) 266–8; *RCSF* 12 (1957) 90–107]

POPKIN, R. H: continuation of 1953 article (see 1953).

RUHE, E. 'Hume and Johnson', *Notes & Queries* 199, 477–8.

STÄDLIN, A. E. *Die Entwicklung der Quantitätstheorie von Cantillon und Hume bis Ricardo*, ch. 3 (121–38). Zürich (diss.) Wintherthur.

WAND, B. *Hume's theory of social and moral motivation*. Cornell U. (diss.).

WOLIN, S. S. 'Hume and Conservatism', *Am. Polit. Sci. Rev.* 48, 999–1016. (repr. 1976 in Livingston & King, *Hume: A Re-evaluation*)

[1955]

GARRIGOU-LAGRANGE, R. 'Le scepticisme empirique de Hume', *Doctor Communis* 8, 149–58.

GOODMAN, N. *Fact, Fiction, and Forecast*, ch. 3, sec. 1 ('The Old Problem of Induction'). London.

GREENBERG, L. 'Necessity in Hume's Causal Theory', *Rev. Met.* 8, 612–23.

GRENE, M. 'David Hume', *Encounter* (March), 54–60. (cf. Grene 1966)

HEDENIUS, I. 'Det tragiska', in Hedenius, *Fyra dygder*, 161–93. Stockholm.

HENDEL, C. W. *David Hume, An Inquiry Concerning Human Understanding*. New York. (with the *Abstract*)
[*M* 67 (1958) 416–19]

LEROY, A.-L. 'David Hume on Criticism', *Erasmus* 8, 648–9. (on Brunius 1952)

MATHUR, G. B. 'Hume and Kant in Their Relation to the Pragmatic Movement', *J. Hist. Ideas* 16, 198–208.

PENELHUM, T. 'Hume on Personal Identity', *Phil. Rev.* 64, 571–89. (repr. 1965 in Sesonske & Fleming, *Human Understanding*; 1966 in Chappell, *Hume*; 1970 in Morick, *Introduction to the Philosophy of Mind*)

POPKIN, R.H. 'The Skeptical Precursors of David Hume',
Phil. & phenomenol. Res. 16, 61–71.

RABBITTE, E. 'Hume's Critique of the Argument From Design',
Phil. Studies (Irel.) 5, 100–17.

ROHMER, J. 'La priorité de l'intentionnalité intellectuelle sur
l'intentionnalité sensible chez Hume', *Revue des sciences
religieuses* 29, 19–44.

ROTWEIN, E. *David Hume: Writings on Economics*.
(cxi, 224 pp.) Edinburgh. (repr. 1970, Madison; 1972,
Freeport, N.Y.)
[*J. polit. Econ.* 64 (1956) 446–7; Arkin 1956;
Philol. Q. 36 (1957) 374–5; *M* 66 (1957) 268;
P 32 (1957) 178; *Eng. Hist. Rev.* 72 (1957) 755–6]

USHENKO, A. 'Hume's Theory of General Ideas', *Rev. Met.* 9,
236–51.

VERGEZ, A. 'Hume, lecteur de Pascal', *Ann. litt. de Franche-
Comté* 2, 27–32.

VLACHOS, G. *Essai sur la politique de Hume*. (247 pp.)
Athens & Paris. [*West. polit. Q.* 9 (1956) 213–14]

WAND, B. 'A Note on Sympathy in Hume's Moral Theory',
Phil. Rev. 64, 275–9.

WATLING, J. 'Inference from the Known to the Unknown',
Proc. Arist. Soc. 55, 83–108.

[1956]

ANCESCHI, L. D. *Hume e i presupposti empiristici della estetica
kantiana*. (202 pp.) Milan.

ARKIN, M. 'The Economic Writings of David Hume—A
Reassessment', *S. Afr. J. Econ.* 24, 204–20. (on Rotwein 1955)
(repr. 1960 in J. J. Spengler & W. R. Allen, *Essays in Economic
Thought*)

AYER, A. J. 'What is a Law of Nature ?', *Revue int. Phil.* 10,
144–65. (repr. 1963 in his *The Concept of A Person*; also 1974
in T. L. Beauchamp, *Philosophical Problems of Causation*,
Encino & Belmont)

BRALY, E. B. *The reputation of David Hume in America*.
Ann Arbor (microfilm).

BRUNIUS, T. *David Hume. Människan och filosofen*. (154 pp.)
Stockholm.

CAMPBELL, C. A. 'Self-activity and its Modes', in H. D. Lewis,
Contemporary British Philosophy (Third Series), esp. 90–9.
London & New York.

CHURCHILL, J. M. *Moral judgment and self-knowledge.* Ann Arbor (microfilm).

CORSI, M. *Elementi logici del primo libro del 'Trattato' di David Hume.* Pisa.

FAY, C. R. *Adam Smith and the Scotland of his day,* passim. Cambridge.

GLATHE, A. B. 'Hume, David', in V. Ferm, *Encyclopedia of Morals* (229–37). New York.

HALBERSTADT, W. H. *The aesthetics of Francis Hutcheson and David Hume.* U. of Illinois (diss.).

HIPPLE, W. J., JR. 'The Logic of Hume's Essay "Of Tragedy"', *Phil. Q.* 6, 43–52.

HURLBUTT, R. H. 'David Hume and Scientific Theism', *J. Hist. Ideas* 17, 486–97.

JØRGENSEN, C. 'On the Possibility of Deducing What Ought to be from What Is', *Ethics* 66, 271–8.

JOHNSTONE, H. W. 'Hume's Arguments concerning Causal Necessity', *Phil. & phenomenol. Res.* 16, 331–40.

KRUSE, A. 'Hume, David', in *Handwörterbuch der Sozial-wissenschaften* (vol. 5, 160–3). Stuttgart, etc.

LEGER, D. 'Bulletin d'histoire de la philosophie moderne', *Revue Sci. phil. & théol.* 40, 542–52.

MARCUS, A. & OCHSNER, B. *Livsanskuelse gennen tiderne.* Bd. 7: *Det 18 århundrede* ... Copenhagen.

MATSON, W. I. 'On the Irrelevance of Free-will to Moral Responsibility, and the Vacuity of the Latter', *Mind* 65, 489–97.

MOSSNER, E. C. 'Hume: the voice of the Enlightenment', in R.P. McCutcheon, *The Present-Day Relevance of Eighteenth-Century Thought.* Washington, D.C.

NEMETZ, A. 'David Hume and John Scotus Eriugena: alternatives in empiricism', *Proc. Am. cath. phil. Ass.* 30, 102–12.

PATRELLE, J. *L'Activité spirituelle chez Berkeley et chez Hume.* Paris (diss.).

PETROVIĆ, G. 'Problem spoznaje u filozofiji D. Hjuma', concluding essay in *Istraživanje o ljudskom razumu* (transl. of the first *Inquiry*). Zagreb.

ROOT, H. E. *David Hume, The Natural History of Religion.* London. [*P* 35 (1960) 85–6]

RYLE, G. 'Hume (1711–1776)', in M. Merleau-Ponty, *Les philosophes célèbres,* 206–9. (transl. as Ryle 1971). Paris.

SIDDIQUI, Z. A. 'Causal argument in Hume's *Dialogues*', *Phil. Q.* (India) 29, 97–100.

TAYLOR, W. L. 'Eighteenth-century Scottish Political
Economy: The Impact on Adam Smith and his Work, of his
Association with Francis Hutcheson and David Hume',
S. Afr. J. Econ. 24, 261–76.

WAND, B. 'Hume's Account of Obligation', *Phil. Q.* 6, 155–68.
(repr. 1966 in Chappell, *Hume*)

[**1957**]

ADAIR, D. '"That Politics may be Reduced to a Science":
David Hume, James Madison, and the Tenth *Federalist*',
Huntington Libr. Q. 20, 343–60. (repr. 1976 in
Livingston & King, *Hume: A Re-evaluation*)

BOAS, G. *Dominant Themes of Modern Philosophy*, 217–29.
New York.

BUTTS, R. E. *Husserl's criticisms of Hume's theory of knowledge.*
U. of Pennsylvania (diss.). (repr. 1976, Ann Arbor & London)

CARLINI, A. 'Hume, David', in *Enciclopedia Filosofica* (vol. 2,
1128–44). Venice. (2nd edn 1967)

CHENTRENS, R. C. & MASSARON, L. 'Il fenomenismo in
Hume', *Pensiero* 2, 108–16.

DAVIS, J. W. *Imagism in Locke, Berkeley, and Hume*, ch. 5
(368–474). Boston U. (diss.).

HALLIE, P. P. 'Hume, Biran and the *méditatifs intérieurs*',
J. Hist. Ideas 18, 295–312. (included, with minor changes,
in the Introduction and ch. 4 of Hallie 1959)

HEIDE, J. E. *Entwertung der Kausalität? Für und wider den
Positivismus.* Stuttgart.

HENDEL, C. W. *David Hume, An Inquiry Concerning the
Principles of Morals.* New York.
[*M* 67 (1958) 416–19; *E* 68 (1958) 147–9]

HIPPLE, W. J., JR. *The Beautiful, The Sublime, & The
Picturesque in Eighteenth-Century British Aesthetic Theory*,
ch 3. Carbondale, Ill.

KEYWORTH, D. R. *The status of theological first principles
according to Hume and Kant.* Ohio State U. (diss.).

MCGLYNN, J. V. 'The two scepticisms in Hume's *Treatise*',
The Thomist 30, 417–46.

MCPHERSON, T. 'The Argument from Design', *Philosophy* 32,
219–28.

MATSON, W. I. 'Hume y el libre albedrío', *Boletino
Informativo del Seminario de Derecho Politico*, U. de
Salamanca, 49–57.

POPPER, K.R. 'Philosophy of Science: A Personal Report', in
C.A. Mace, *British Philosophy in the Mid-Century*, 155–91.
London. (repr. 1963 in Popper, *Conjectures and Refutations*,
33–65, London. The section on Hume is also repr. in
Sesonske & Fleming 1965)

PRETI, G. *Alle origini dell'etica contemporanea. Adamo Smith.*
Bari.
[*RFNS* 50 (1958) 554–7]

SUGG, R.S., JR. 'Hume's Search for the Key with the
Leathern Thong', *J. Aesth. & Art Crit.* 16, 96–102.

VICKERS, D. 'Method and Analysis in David Hume's Economic
Essays', *Economica* 24, 225–34.

VON LEYDEN, W., 'Hume and "Imperfect Identity"',
Phil. Q. 7, 340–52.

WARNOCK, H.M.; EWING, A.C. 'The Justification of
Emotions', *Proc. Arist. Soc.* suppl. vol.31, 43–74.

[**1958**]

ASPELIN, G. *Tankens vägar: en översikt av filosofiens utveckling*,
pt.2, 141–53. Stockholm.

BAIER, K. *The Moral Point of View*, ch.11. (repr. 1976 in
J. Glickman, *Moral Philosophy: An Introduction*,
New York & London) [*Sth. J. Phil.* 2 (1965) 127–30]

BARONE, F. '1748: Viaggio di Hume a Torino', *Filosofia* 9,
616–32.

BASSON, A.H. *David Hume*. Harmondsworth. (for reprint see
Cavendish 1968)
[*M* 68 (1959) 570–1; *JP* 56 (1959) 545–50;
PR 69 (1960) 265–7; *P* 35 (1960) 274–5; *PQ* 10 (1960)
275–9]

BONGIE, L.L. 'David Hume and the Official Censorship of the
Ancien Régime', *French Studies* 12, 234–46.

BROWN, T.J. 'English Literary Autographs XXVI. George
Berkeley... David Hume...'. *Book Collector* 7, 191.

COHEN, R. 'David Hume's Experimental Method and the
Theory of Taste', *Engl. lit. Hist.* 25, 270–89.

FRIEDRICH, C.J. *The Philosophy of Law in Historical
Perspective*, ch.11. Chicago.

HOCHFELDOWA, A. 'Miejsce krytyki religii w filozofii Dawida
Hume'a', *Sprawozdania z Prac Naukowych Wydziatu Nauk
Spolecznych PAN* 7, 68–72.

JACOBSON, N.P. 'Hume on the Uses of Reason in Religion',
Iliff Rev. 15, 49–59.

LAZEROWITZ, M. 'Moore and Philosophical Analysis', *Philosophy* 33, 193–220. (repr. 1964 as ch. 4 of Lazerowitz, *Studies in Metaphilosophy*, London) [*P* 35 (1960) 151–3]

LENZ, J. W. 'Hume's Defense of Causal Inference', *J. Hist. Ideas* 19, 559–67. (repr. 1966 in Chappell, *Hume*)

MAYO, B. *Ethics and the Moral Life*, 83–9. London.

MEYER, P. H. 'Voltaire and Hume as Historians: A comparative study of the *Essai sur les moeurs* and the *History of England*', *PMLA* 73, 51–68.

MICHALENKO, J. P. 'K kritičeskoj ocenke dejstvitel'nogo istoričeskogo značenija filosofskich vzgljadov Davida Juma', *USSR Acad. Sci.*

MICHALENKO, J. P. 'O nepravil'noj ocenke filosofii Juma', *Vopr. filosofii* 11, 177–218.

MICHALENKO, J. P. 'Ob ocenke dejstvitel'nogo istoričeskogo značenija teorii pričinnosti Juma', *Filosofskie Nauki* 2, 172–83.

MILLER, C. 'A Middle Course for Ethicists', *Ethics* 68, 207–9.

MOSSNER, E. C. 'Hume at La Flèche, 1735: An Unpublished Letter', *Studies in English* 37, 30–3.

MULLINS, W. J. *The political philosophy of David Hume.* U. of Calif., Berkeley (diss.).

PAP, A. *Semantics and Necessary Truth . . .*, ch. 4. New Haven. (Spanish transl. 1970)

STACE, W. T. 'Some Misinterpretations of Empiricism', *Mind* 67, 465–84. [*Theoria* 29 (1963) 290–303]

TENKKU, J. 'Tosiasia—ja arvoarvostelma Humen filosofiassa' (Judgment of fact and value in Hume's philosophy), *Ajatus* 20, 259–73.

TODD, W. B. 'Hume, *Exposé Succinct*', *Book Collector* 7, 181.

WESTON, J. C., JR. 'A Fragment of a New Letter by David Hume in Defence of his *History of England*', *Notes & Queries* 203, 476–7.

WOITYTA, C. Article in Polish on the role of reason in ethics according to Aquinas, Hume, and Kant, in *Roczniki Filozoficzne Towarzystwa Naukowego Katolickiego Uniwersytetu Lubelskiego* 6. (Lublin)

ZABEEH, F. *The place of meaning and reason in Hume's theory of knowledge.* U. of Calif., Berkeley (diss.).

[**1959**]

BAXTER, I. F. G. 'David Hume and Justice', *Revue int. Phil.* 13, 112–31.

BUNGE, M. *Causality*, 42–62. Cambridge, Mass.

BUTCHVAROV, P. 'The Self and Perceptions; A study in Humean Philosophy', *Phil. Q.* 9, 97–115.
[*PQ* 26 (1976) 42–4]

BUTTS, R. E. 'Hume's Scepticism', *J. Hist. Ideas* 20, 413–19.

BUTTS, R. E. 'Husserl's Critique of Hume's Notion of *Distinctions of Reason*', *Phil. & phenomenol. Res.* 20, 213–21.

CAMERON, J. M. 'Miracles', *The Month*, 286–97.

CAMPANALE, D. 'L'ambivalenza gnoseologica ed epistemologica dell'empirismo critico di Hume', *Annali della Facoltà di Lett. e Fil. dell' U. di Bari* 5. (repr. in Campanale 1961)

CHRISTIAN, W. A. *An Interpretation of Whitehead's Metaphysics*, ch. 8. New Haven.

CLIVE, G. 'Hume's *Dialogues* Reconsidered', *J. Relig.* 39, 110–19.

COLLINS, J. *God in Modern Philosophy*, ch. 4. Chicago.

COPLESTON, F. *A History of Philosophy*, vol. 5, chs. 14–18. London.

DAVIES, G. 'Hume's History of the Reign of James I', in Herbert Davis & Helen Gardner, *Elizabethan and Jacobean Studies, Presented to Frank Percy Wilson . . .* , 231–49. Oxford.

EASTERLING, M. L. *Hume's theory of moral judgment.* U. of Illinois (diss.).

ESTALL, H. M. 'Hume's "Ruling Passion" ', *Queen's Q.* 66, 46–55.

FLEW, A. 'Hume and "the Religious Hypothesis" ' *Rationalist Annual*, 34–43. (cf. Flew 1961, ch. 9) (repr. 1976 in his *The Presumption of Atheism*)

FLEW, A. 'Hume's Check', *Phil. Q.* 9, 1–18. (mostly absorbed into Flew 1961, ch. 8)

HALLIE, P. P. *Maine de Biran: Reformer of empiricism*, chs. 3–5. Cambridge, Mass.

HART, H. L. A. & HONORÉ, A. M. *Causation in the Law*, ch. 1. Oxford.

HAYMOND, W. S. *Hume's theory of sense perception.* St. Louis U. (diss.).

JACOBSON, N. P. 'The Uses of Reason in Religion: A Note on David Hume', *J. Relig.* 39, 103–9, [40 (1960) 40–2]

KROOK, D. *Three Traditions of Moral Thought*, ch. 6. Cambridge.

LUCAS, F. L. *The Art of Living; Four eighteenth-century minds*, 1–78. London.

MacIntyre, A. C. 'Hume on "Is" and "Ought"', *Phil. Rev.*
68, 451–68. (repr. 1966 in Chappell, *Hume*; 1969 in Hudson,
The Is–Ought Question; 1971 in MacIntyre, *Against the
Self-Images of the Age*)
[*PR* 70 (1961) 231–44; *P* 48 (1973) 277–83]

Manuel, F. E. *The Eighteenth Century Confronts the Gods*,
168–83. Cambridge, Mass.

Maxwell, J. C. 'Hume: A Reference to Pope', *Notes & Queries*
204, 404. [*NQ* 205 (1960) 115]

Mossner, E. C. 'Did Hume Ever Read Berkeley?
A Rejoinder to Professor Popkin', *J. Phil.* 56, 992–5.

Popkin, R. H. 'Did Hume Ever Read Berkeley?', *J. Phil.* 56,
535–45.

Pustilnik, J. *Process and causality: Whitehead's reply to Hume.*
Columbia U. (diss.).

Rescher, N. 'Logical Analysis in Historical Application'
(to Hume's *Dialogues*, pt. ix), *Methodos* 11, 1–8.
(repr. 1969 in Rescher, *Essays in Philosophical Analysis*,
Pittsburgh)

Stiehler, G. 'Das Humesche Induktionsproblem und seine
Lösung durch den dialektischen Materialismus', *Dtsch. Z.
Phil.* 7, 432–44.

Sweigart, J. W. *The epistemological status of ethical
statements for D. Hume and C.I. Lewis.* U. of Pennsylvania
(diss.).

Tanaka, T. 'David Hume no kakei-gaikoku-boeki ron'
(Hume's theories on money and foreign trade),
Keizaigaku Ronkyū 13, no. 3.

Tanaka, T. 'David Hume no keizai riron' (Economic theory
of David Hume), *Keizaigaku Ronkyū* 13, no. 2.

Tranøy, K. E. 'Hume on Morals, Animals, and Men',
J. Phil. 56, 94–103.

Waber, W. F. *The roles of reason and sentiment in Hume's
doctrine of the social virtues.* Johns Hopkins U. (diss.).

Wedberg, A. *Filosofins Historia*, vol. 2. chs. 4–5. Stockholm.

Wenzel, L. *David Humes politische Philosophie in ihrem
Zusammenhang mit seiner gesamten Lehre.* Cologne.

Wiener, P. P. 'Did Hume Ever Read Berkeley?', *J. Phil.* 56,
533–5. [535–45; 992–5]

Životić, M. *Hume* [transliterated]. (32 pp.) Belgrade.

ARMSTRONG, D. M. *Berkeley's Theory of Vision*, 87–102. Melbourne.

ATKINSON, R. F. 'Hume on Mathematics', *Phil. Q.* 10, 127–37.

BECK, L. W. *Six Secular Philosophers*, ch. 4. New York.

BUTLER, R. J. 'Natural Belief and the Enigma of Hume', *Arch. Gesch. Phil.* 42, 73–100. [*P* 49 (1974) 281–94]

CASTIGNONE, S. 'La Dottrina della Giustizia in David Hume', *Riv. int. Fil. Diritto* 37, 457–95.

COULTER, C. L. *Language and analysis in the philosophy of David Hume*. Harvard U. (diss.).

DUCASSE, C. J. 'David Hume on Causation', in R. M. Blake et al., *Theories of Scientific Method: The Renaissance through the Nineteenth Century*, ch. 7 (144–52). Seattle.

GLOSSOP, R. J. *A critical analysis of some aspects of C. L. Stevenson's ethical theory*. Washington U. (St Louis) (diss.).

GOSSMAN, L. 'Berkeley, Hume, and Maupertuis', *French Studies* 14, 304–24.

GOSSMAN, L. 'Two Unpublished Essays on Mathematics in the Hume Papers', *J. Hist. Ideas* 21, 442–9.

GRAVE, S. A. *The Scottish Philosophy of Common Sense*, esp. ch. 2. Oxford.

HUNTER, G. 'David Hume: Some Unpublished Letters, 1771–1776', *Texas Studies in Lit. & Lang.* 2, 127–50.

JESSOP, T. E. 'Réflexions sur la philosophie de Hume', *Revue phil.* 85, 185–96.

MACNABB, D. G. C. 'Hume, David', in J. O. Urmson, *The Concise Encyclopaedia of Western Philosophy and Philosophers* (166–8 and 185–8). London. (2nd edn 1975)

MINKUS, P. A. *Philosophy of the Person*, 22–34. Oxford.

MOSSNER, E. C. ' "Of the Principle of Moral Estimation: A Discourse between David Hume, Robert Clerk, and Adam Smith"; An Unpublished MS by Adam Ferguson', *J. Hist. Ideas* 21, 222–32.

NAESS, S. & A. 'Psychological Research and Humean problems', *Phil. Sci.* 27, 134–46.

NOYES, C. E. 'Hume's "Umbrage to the Godly" ', in his *History of England*', *U. of Mississippi Studies in English* 1, 86–96.

O'DONNELL, M. 'Hume's Approach to Causation', *Phil. Studies* (Irel.) 10, 64–99.

PRICE, J. V. *The Dialogues of Hume and Cicero on natural religion*. U. of Texas (diss.).

RORTY, A. O. *Self-reference and the theory of error: Descartes, Hume, and Bradley on philosophic method.* Yale U. (diss.).

SMITH, J. W. See Ward Smith.

VON LEYDEN, W. 'Existence: A Humean point in Aristotle's *Metaphysics'*, *Rev. Met.* 13, 597–604.

WARD SMITH, J. 'Concerning Hume's Intentions', *Phil. Rev.* 69, 63–77.

WASSERSTROM, R. 'Hume and Philosophical Analysis: A Reply to Professor Lazerowitz', *Philosophy* 35, 151–3. (on Lazerowitz 1958)

WOLFF, R. P. 'Hume's Theory of Mental Activity', *Phil. Rev.* 69, 289–310. (repr. 1966 in Chappell, *Hume*)

WOLFF, R. P. 'Kant's Debt to Hume via Beattie', *J. Hist. Ideas* 21, 117–23.

WOLFSON, H. A. 'The Philonic God of Revelation and his latter-day deniers', *Harvard theol. Rev.* 53, 101–24.

ZABEEH, F. *Hume, Precursor of Modern Empiricism.* The Hague. [*PB* (1961) 21–2; *PQ* 13 (1963) 81–2; *PR* 72 (1963) 260–1; *AGP* 45 (1963) 94–7; *Erasmus* 15 (1963) 653–8; *JVI* 5 (1971) 75–7]

ZABEEH, F. 'Hume's Scepticism with Regard to Deductive Reason', *Ratio* 2, 134–43. (repr. 1960, with some omissions, as ch. 5 of the preceding)

[1961]

AMBACHER, M. 'Existe-t-il en dehors des sciences de l'homme une connaissance proprement philosophique de la nature humaine ?', *Études philosophiques* 16, 183–7.

ARMSTRONG, D. M. *Perception and the Physical World*, ch. 4. London.

ASCHENBRENNER, K. 'Psychologism in Hume', *Phil. Q.* 11, 28–38.

ATKINSON, R. F. 'Hume on "Is" and "Ought": A Reply to Mr. MacIntyre', *Phil. Rev.* 70, 231–8. (on MacIntyre 1959) (repr. 1966 in Chappell, *Hume*; 1969 in Hudson, *The Is–Ought Question*)

BLACKSTONE, W. T. 'Hume and Ritschlian Theology', *The Personalist* 42, 561–70.

BLANSHARD, B. *Reason and Goodness*, ch. 4 ('The Dialectic of Reason and Feeling in British Ethics'). London.

BONGIE, L. L. 'Hume: *Philosophe* and Philosopher in Eighteenth-Century France', *French Studies* 15, 213–27.

BRACKEN, H. M. 'Locke, Berkeley, Hume: The end of a triumvirate', *Indian J. Phil.* 3, 1–8. (also 1960 in *Rev. Fil. de la U. de Costa Rica* 2, 351–5)

BROAD, C. D. 'Hume's Doctrine of Space', *Proc. Br. Acad.* 47, 161–76.

CAMPANALE, D. *Problemi epistemologici, da Hume all'ultimo Wittgenstein*. Bari.

CRANSTON, M. 'Rousseau in England', *Hist. Today* 11, 599–606. [793]

FLEW, A. 'Did Hume Ever Read Berkeley ?', *J. Phil.* 58, 50–1. [207–9; 327–8]

FLEW, A. *Hume's Philosophy of Belief: A study of his first 'Inquiry'*. London & New York.
[*Blackfriars* 43 (1962) 182–5; *JP* 59 (1962) 439–45; *PR* 72 (1963) 261–3; *PQ* 13 (1963) 367–8; *AJP* 41 (1963) 427–32; *P* 39 (1964) 88–90; *M* 74 (1965) 299–300; *JHP* 3 (1965) 128–31]

FLEW, A. 'Miracle and History', *Listener* 65, 963–4.

FLEW, A. 'Philosopher of the Enlightenment', *Guardian*, 26 Apr., 10.

FRENCH, S. G. 'Hume's Hurdle', *J. Phil.* 58, 710–11. (abstract of French 1963)

FURLONG, E. J. 'Imagination in Hume's *Treatise* and *Enquiry Concerning the Human Understanding*', *Philosophy* 36, 62–70. (repr. 1961 as part [95–105] of ch. 10 of the following)

FURLONG, E. J. *Imagination*, 62–8 (belief in body) and ch. 10 (95–113). London.

GRIMSLEY, R. 'A French correspondent of David Hume: Fenouillot de Falbaire', *Mod. Lang. Rev.* 56, 561–3.

GRIMSLEY, R. 'D'Alembert and Hume', *Revue Litt. comp.* 35, 583–5.

GRUBEL, H. G. 'Ricardo and Thornton on the Transfer Mechanism', *Q. J. Econ.* 75, 292–301.

HAMLYN, D. W. *Sensation and Perception: A history of the philosophy of perception*, esp. ch. 6, sec. 4. London.

HARTSHORNE, C. 'Hume's Metaphysics and its Present-Day Influence', *New Scholasticism* 35, 152–71.

HEYWOOD, L. J. G. 'Genteel Office: David Hume—Librarian', *Scottish Libr. Ass. News* 50, 10–11.

KNEALE, W. 'Universality and Necessity', *Br. J. Phil. Sci.* 12, 89–102. (repr. 1974 in T. L. Beauchamp, *Philosophical Problems of Causation*, Encino & Belmont)

LEHMANN-LEANDER, E. B. *Hume und Kant, das Erkenntnisproblem: Quellen zur Erkenntnistheorie*. Frankfurt.

LOVEJOY, A. O. *Reflections on Human Nature*, Lectures 5 and 8. Baltimore.

LOZIER, C. 'David Hume: flight from abstraction', *Dominicana* 46, 234–47.

MONTAGUE-SMITH, P. W. 'Ancestry of David Hume the Philosopher', *Genealogists' Mag.* 13, 274–9.

MÜNZ, T. 'David Hume', *Otázky marxistickej Filozofie* 16, 370–3.

NOXON, J. 'Hume's Opinion of Critics', *J. Aesth. & Art Crit.* 20, 157–62.

ROBINSON, D. S. *The Story of Scottish Philosophy*, ch. 2. New York. (anthol.)

SCHAEFER, A. *Erkenntnis, menschliche Natur und Bild des politischen Menschen in der Philosophie David Humes.* Berlin-Dahlem (diss.).

SCHIPPER, E. W. 'Kant's Answer to Hume's Problem', *Kant-Studien* 53, 68–74. [56 (1965) 71–8]

SCOTT-TAGGART, M. J. 'MacIntyre's Hume', *Phil. Rev.* 70, 239–44. (on MacIntyre 1959) (repr. 1969 in Hudson, *The Is–Ought Question*)

SPROTT, S. E. *The English Debate on Suicide, from Donne to Hume*, esp. 128–34. La Salle, Ill.

SULLIVAN, C. J. 'Spinoza and Hume on causation', *Atti del XII Congr. int. Fil.* (Venice), vol. 12, 431–7. Florence.

SWABEY, W. C. *Ethical Theory from Hobbes to Kant*, ch. 9. New York.

TEDESCHI, P. 'Paradoxe de l'explication des idées résultant de leur double caractère de relation et de séparation dans l'associationisme de Hume', in Tedeschi, *Paradoxe de la pensée anglaise au XVIIIᵉ siècle ou l'ambiguité du sens commun*, 129–68. Paris.

TREVOR-ROPER, H. R. 'David Hume as a Historian', *Listener* 66, 1103–4. (repr. 1963 in Pears, *David Hume*)

TSUGAWA, A. 'David Hume and Lord Kames on Personal Identity', *J. Hist. Ideas* 22, 398–403.

WIENER, P. P. 'Did Hume Ever Read Berkeley?', *J. Phil.* 58, 207–9 and 327–8. [61 (1964) 773–8]

ZABEEH, F. 'Hume on Metaphysics and the Limits of Human Knowledge', *Theoria* 27, 12–25. (also printed as pp. 24–36 of his book, 1960)

ALLARD, J.-L. 'L'explication empiriste de la causalité selon David Hume', *Revue de l'Univ. d'Ottawa* 32, 153–67.

APPLETON, E. et al. *David Hume. 250th Anniversary of the Birth of David Hume: 1711–1961. A Record of the Commemoration.* Edinburgh.

ÁRDAL, P. S. 'Passion and Value in Hume's *Treatise*', in Appleton, 16–20.

BENARDETE, J. A. 'Is there a Problem about Logical Possibility ?', *Mind* 71, 342–52.

BITZER, L. F. *The lively idea: a study of Hume's influence on George Campbell's 'Philosophy of Rhetoric'.* U. of Iowa (diss.).

BLANSHARD, B. *Reason and Analysis*, ch. 11 ('Necessity in Causation'). La Salle, Ill.

BLAUG, M. *Economic Theory in Retrospect*, ch. 1. Homewood, Ill. (2nd edn London 1968)

CARNEY, J. D. 'Malcolm and Moore's Rebuttals', *Mind* 71, 353–63.

CASTIGNONE, G. 'Diritto Naturale e Diritto Positivo in David Hume', *Riv. int. Fil. Diritto* 39, 79–82.

COHEN, R. 'The Transformation of Passion: A Study of Hume's Theories of Tragedy', *Philol. Q.* 41, 450–64.

COURTNEY, C. P. 'David Hume et l'Abbé Raynal: Une source de l'*Histoire philosophique des deux Indes*', *Revue Litt. comp.* 36, 565–71.

CRANSTON, M. 'Rousseau's Visit to England, 1766–67', *Trans. R. Soc. Lit. U.K.* 31, 16–34. London.

DAVIE, G. E. 'Hume in His Contemporary Setting', in Appleton, 11–15.

DEAN, E. 'Hume on Religious Language', *J. Relig.* 42, 44–51.

DÜR, S. 'Reid jako krytyk epistemologii Hume'a' [Article in Polish on Reid's criticism of Hume's epistemology], *Studia Filozoficzne* 29, 117–43.

ELLIS, F. R. *Hume's theory of nature.* St Louis U. (diss.).

FINLAYSON, C. P. 'David Hume Exhibition' (a catalogue of books and MSS displayed), in Appleton, 29–39.

FLEW, A. *Hume on Human Nature and the Understanding.* New York. (anthol.)
[*Hermathena* no. 99 (1964) 118–19]

FORMIGARI, L. *L'estetica del gusto nel settecento inglese*, esp. chs. 5 and 7. Florence.

GIARRIZZO, G. *David Hume Politico e Storico.* Turin.
[*Hist. & Theory* 3 (1963), 381–9; *Cambridge hist. J.* 6 (1963) 280–95]

GRIMSLEY, R. 'Concerning an unpublished note from Morellet to Hume', *Mod. Lang. Rev.* 57, 65–7.

HAMPSHIRE, S. 'David Hume's Place in Philosophy', *Listener* 67, 1063–4. (repr. 1963 in Pears, *David Hume*)

HOCHFELDOWA, A. *D. Hume: Dialogii o religii naturalnej; Naturalna historia religii.* Warsaw.
[*Przegląd Kulturalny* 43 (1962) 9; *Argumenty* 11 (1963) 11]

HORN, D.B. 'Hume as Historian', in Appleton, 25–8.

HUNTER, G.B.B. 'Hume on *Is* and *Ought*', *Philosophy* 37, 148–52. (repr. 1969 in Hudson, *The Is-Ought Question*)
[*P* 38 (1963) 178–84; *PQ* 14 (1964) 246–52]

JØRGENSEN, C. 'The Relation Is/Ought. Hume's Problem', *Theoria* 28, 53–69.

KATZ, J.J. *The Problem of Induction and Its Solution*, ch. 3. Chicago.

KRAUSSER, P. 'Humes Problem in kybernetischer Perspektive', *Philosophia Naturalis* 7, 451–74.

MACDIARMID, H. *The Man of almost Independent Mind.* (11 pp.) Edinburgh.

MCDONALD, L.C. *Western Political Theory: The Modern Age*, ch. 8 (218–35). Burlingame, N.Y.

MACNABB, D.G.C. *David Hume, A Treatise of Human Nature, Book One.* London.

MICHALENKO, J.P. Философия Д. Юма — теоретическая английского позитивизма XX века. (149 pp.) Moscow.

MILLER, E. 'David Hume: Whig or Tory ?', *New Individualist Rev.* 1.

MOLINARI, E. 'Diritto e linguaggio in Hume', *Riv. int. Fil. Diritto* 39, 400–2.

MOLINARI, E. 'Passioni e ragione nella concezione etica e giuridica di Hume', *Annali della Fac. di Giurisprudenza, Univ. di Genova*, 394–414.

MOSSNER, E.C. 'New Hume Letters to Lord Elibank, 1748–1776' *Texas Studies in Lit. & Lang.* 4, 431–60.

NELSON, L. *Fortschritte und Rückschritte der Philosophie von Hume und Kant bis Hegel und Fries.* Frankfurt am Main. (Engl. transl. 1970: see Nelson 1970)

NOYES, C.E. 'Samuel Johnson: student of Hume', *U. of Mississippi Studies in Engl.* 3, 91–4.

POMEROY, R.S. 'Hume on the Testimony for Miracles', *Speech Monographs* 29, 1–12.

ROBINSON, J. A. 'Hume's Two Definitions of "Cause"',
Phil. Q. 12, 162–71. (repr. 1966 in Chappell, *Hume,* with a
reply to criticism, 162–8.)
[*PQ* 15 (1965) 247–53; 21 (1971) 168–71; *AGP* 55 (1973)
287–300]

SULLIVAN, C. J. 'David Hume on the understanding',
Augustinianum 2, 88–114 and 285–302 and 507–18.

WAND, B. 'Hume's Non-Utilitarianism', *Ethics* 72, 193–6.

WINCH, D. N. 'The Place of Hume in the History of Economic
Thought', in Appleton, 21–5.

WINKS, R. W. 'Hume and Gibbon: A View from a Vantage',
Dalhousie Rev. 41, 496–504.

[1963]

ANON. 'The Grave Memorials of Famous Men and Women.
2—David Hume' (Old Calton Cemetery, Edinburgh),
Monumental J. 30, 14–17.

BENNETT, J. F. 'The Status of Determinism', *Br. J. Phil. Sci.* 14,
106–19.

BROILES, R. D. *An analysis of Hume's arguments concerning the
role of reason in moral decisions.* Ohio State U. (diss.).

CAIN, R. E. *David Hume and Adam Smith: a study in intellectual
kinship.* Austin, Tex. (diss.).

CHAPPELL, V. C. *The Philosophy of David Hume.* (lxx, 596 pp.)
(The Modern Library of the world's best books) New York.
(anthol.) (contains selections from the *Treatise* and the
Inquiries, and the complete *Dialogues,* etc.)

COX, K. B. *Hume's theory of moral judgments in the 'Treatise'.*
U. of Michigan (diss.).

EWING, A. C. 'The Alleged Contradiction in Hume',
Philosophy 38, 370.

FLEW, A. 'On the Interpretation of Hume', *Philosophy* 38,
178–82. (on Hunter 1962) (repr. 1966 in Chappell, *Hume*;
1969 in Hudson, *The Is-Ought Question*) [*P* 38 (1963) 182–4]

FOOT, P. R. 'Hume on Moral Judgement', in Pears, 67–76.

FORBES, D. 'Politics and History in David Hume', *Camb.
hist. J.* 6, 280–95. (on Giarrizzo 1962)

FRENCH, S. G. 'Hume's Hurdle', *Dialogue* 1, 390–9.

GARDINER, P. L. 'Hume's Theory of the Passions', in Pears,
31–42.

GILSON, E. & LANGAN, T. *Modern Philosophy: Descartes to
Kant,* ch. 16. New York.
[*PR* 75 (1966) 112–13; *RM* 18 (1964) 293–300]

HAYEK, F.A. 'The Legal and Political Philosophy of David Hume', *Il Politico* 28, 691–704. (repr. 1966 in Chappell, *Hume*)

HENDEL, C.W. *Studies in the Philosophy of David Hume*, 2nd edn. (1st edn 1925) Indianapolis. (contains Hendel, 'A Review of Hume Scholarship since 1925', on pp. xxi–li; a supplement, 'On Atomism: A Critique of Hume's First Principles and Method', on pp. 379–480; and four appendixes: on Hume's 'discoveries', his relationship to Hutcheson, on space and time, and on the nature of experience.)
[*JHP* 2 (1964) 269 (in French); *D* 3 (1964/5) 299–307]

HILL, R.S. 'David Hume', in Leo Strauss & Joseph Cropsey, *History of Political Philosophy* (509–31). Chicago. (2nd edn 1972)

HUNTER, G.B. 'A Reply to Professor Flew', *Philosophy* 38, 182–4. (on Flew 1963) (repr. 1966 in Chappell, *Hume*, with reply by Flew on pp. 291–4; 1969 in Hudson, *The Is-Ought Question*)

KENNY, A. *Action, Emotion and Will*, 20–8. London.
[*PQ* 26 (1976) 14–23]

KLOCKER, H.R. 'Empiricism and reality', *Heythrop J.* 4, 42–53.

KOZANECKI, T. 'Dawida Hume' a nieznane listy w zbiorach Muzeum Czartoryskich (Polska)', *Archiwum Historii Filozofii i Myśli Społecznej* 9, 127–41.

LINEBACK, R.H. *The place of the imagination in Hume's epistemology*. Bloomington (diss.).

MALL, R.A. *Humes Bild vom Menschen*. (iii, 167 pp.) Cologne. (cf. Mall 1967)

MILES, T.R. See Michotte 1947.

MOLINARI, E. 'Interesse individuale e interesse pubblico in Hume', *Riv. int. Fil. Diritto* 40, 564–82.

MORITZ, M. 'Humes Ansichten über Freiheit und Notwendigkeit', in Joseph Frank et al., *Horizons of a Philosopher: Essays in honor of David Baumgardt*, 315–28. Leiden.

MOSSNER, E.C. *David Hume, An Enquiry concerning Human Understanding, and Other Essays*. New York.

MOSSNER, E.C. 'Adam Ferguson's "Dialogue on a Highland Jaunt" with Robert Adam, William Cleghorn, David Hume, and William Wilkie', in C. Camden, *Restoration and Eighteenth-Century Literature: Essays in Honor of Alan Dugald McKillop*, 297–308. Chicago.

MUCKLER, F. A. 'On the Reason of Animals: Historical Antecedents to the Logic of Modern Behaviorism', *Psychol. Reports* 12, 863–82.

NETHERY, W. 'Hume's Manuscript Corrections in a Copy of *A Treatise of Human Nature*', *Papers of the Biblio. Soc. of America* 57, 446–7. (cf. Connon 1975)

OSSOWSKA, M. 'Dawid Hume jako obserwator i kodyfikator życia moralnego', *Studia Filozoficzne* 32, 129–67.

PEARS, D. F. *David Hume: A Symposium*. London. (includes Pears, 'Hume on Personal Identity', pp. 43–54; repr. 1972 in Hanfling, *Fundamental Problems in Philosophy*; and Pears, 'Hume's Empiricism and Modern Empiricism', pp. 11–30; repr. 1975 in his *Questions in the Philosophy of Mind*; and reprints of Trevor-Roper 1961 and Hampshire 1962)
[*PQ* 15 (1965) 265; *P* 40 (1965) 251–3]

PIKE, N. 'Hume on Evil', *Phil. Rev.* 72, 180–97. (repr. 1964 in Pike, *God and Evil*; 1971 in Weinberg & Yandell, *Problems in Philosophical Inquiry*; 1972 in J. Donnelly, *Logical Analysis & Contemporary Theism*; 1974 in B. Brody, *Readings in the Phil. of Religion*, Englewood Cliffs, N.J.)
[*RS* 6 (1970) 369–77]

PIKE, N. C. *Hume on personal identity*. Harvard U. (diss.).

PLAMENATZ, J. *Man and Society: A critical examination of some important social and political theories from Machiavelli to Marx*, vol. 1, ch. 8 (299–331). London.

POPKIN, R. H. 'Bayle and Hume', in *Trans. XIIIth int. Congr. Phil.* (Mexico City).

POPKIN, R. H. 'Scepticism in the Enlightenment', in *Trans. 1st int. Congr. on the Enlightenment (Studies in Voltaire and the Eighteenth Century)*, 1321–45. Geneva.

PRICE, J. V. 'Empirical Theists in Cicero and Hume', *Texas Studies in Lit. & Lang.* 5, 255–64.

RAO, L. 'A critical note on Hume and philosophical analysis', *Phil. Q.* (India) 36, 9–13.

SANTUCCI, A. *Appunti di critica humiana*. (Lecture). Bologna.

SCHAEFER, A. *David Hume, Philosophie und Politik*. (Monographien zur philosophischen Forschung, 24) Meisenheim am Glan.
[*Biblio. of Phil.* 12 (1965) 344; *Estudios Filosóficos* 14 (1965) 203–4; *Pensamiento* 21 (1965) 200–1; *Phil. Literaturanzeiger* 18 (1965) 26–9]

SHOEMAKER, S. *Self-Knowledge and Self-Identity*, passim. Ithaca.

SINHA, D. 'Phenomenology and Positivism', *Phil. & phenomenol. Res.* 23, 569–77.

SNETHLAGE, J. L. *David Hume.* The Hague.

STEWART, J. B. *The Moral and Political Philosophy of David Hume.* New York & London. (repr. 1973, Westport, Conn.)
[*D* 3 (1964) 308–10; *Am. hist. Rev.* 70 (1964) 119–20; *U. Toronto Q.* 34 (1965) 405–7; *PQ* 16 (1966) 76–7; Cook 1968]

TANAKA, T. 'Kindai shakai no genri o meguru Hume to Wallace' (Hume and Wallace on the structure of modern society), *Keizaigaku Ronkyū* 17, nos. 1 and 3.

VAN LEEUWEN, H. G. *The Problem of Certainty in English Thought, 1630–1690*, 146–52. The Hague.

WALSH, W. H. *Metaphysics*, ch. 7 ('The Limits of Reason: Hume and Causality'). London.

WARNOCK, G. J. 'Hume on Causation', in Pears, 55–66.

WIENER, P. P. 'James Gregory: *On Power*', *J. Hist. Ideas* 24, 241–68. [*JHI* 25 (1964) 128–9]

WILLIAMS, B. A. O. 'Hume on Religion', in Pears, 77–88.

WOLFF, R. P. *Kant's Theory of Mental Activity*, esp. 154–64. Cambridge, Mass.

WOLLHEIM, R. *Hume on Religion.* (*Natural History of Religion, Dialogues*, & various essays) London.

YOLTON, J. W. 'The Concept of Experience in Locke and Hume', *J. Hist. Phil.* 1, 53–71. (part repr. 1968 in C. B. Martin & D. M. Armstrong, *Locke and Berkeley*)

ZABEEH, F. 'Vindication of Hume', *Theoria* 29, 290–303. (on Stace 1958)

[1964]

ALLAIRE, E. B. 'The Attack on Substance: Descartes to Hume', *Dialogue* 3, 284–7.

ÁRDAL, P. S. 'Remarks concerning the Account of the Nature of Moral Evaluation in Hume's *Treatise*', *Philosophy* 39, 341–5. (repr., with minor alterations, within ch. 9 of Árdal 1966)

BALLARD, E. G. 'Renaissance Space and the Humean Development in Philosophical Psychology', *Tulane Studies in Phil.* 13, 55–79.

BONGIE, L. L. 'The Eighteenth-Century Marian Controversy and an Unpublished Letter by David Hume', *Studies in Scottish Lit.* 1, 236–52.

BROILES, D. *The Moral Philosophy of David Hume*. The Hague. (2nd edn 1969)

[*P* 40 (1965) 354–5; *M* 75 (1966) 447–9; *PQ* 16 (1966) 278–80]

BRUNETTO, F. *La questione della 'vera causa' in David Hume*. (viii, 80 pp.) Bologna.

CASTIGNONE, S. 'Criteri di legittimazione del potere politico: contratto e consenso nel pensiero di David Hume', *Riv. int. Fil. Diritto* 41, 185–9.

CASTIGNONE, S. *Giustizia e bene comune in David Hume*. (155 pp.) Milan. [*Stromata* 21 (1965) 537–8]

COCHRANE, J. A. *Dr. Johnson's Printer: The Life of William Strahan*, ch. 5 ('David Hume'). London.

CRAGG, G. R. *Reason and Authority in the Eighteenth Century*, ch. 5. Cambridge.

CROSSNER, P. 'The devolution of ethics. From Hume to Ayer', *Memorias del XIII Congr. int. de Fil.* (Mexico), vol. 7, 257–66. Mexico City.

CURRIE, C. 'Hendel on Hume's Atomism', *Dialogue* 3, 299–307. (on Hendel 1963)

DIETL, P. J. *Explanation and action, an examination of the controversy between Hume and some of his contemporary critics*. Indiana U. (diss.).

DUNN, J. 'Authorship of Gregory's Critique of Hume', *J. Hist. Ideas* 25, 128–9. (on Wiener 1963)

FEIGL, H. 'What Hume Might Have Said to Kant, . . .', in M. A. Bunge, *The Critical Approach to Science and Philosophy*, 45–51. New York.

FLEW, A. G. N. 'Hume', in D. J. O'Connor, *A Critical History of Western Philosophy*, 253–74. London.

FOX, M. 'Religion and Human Nature in the Philosophy of David Hume', in W. L. Reese & E. Freeman, *Process and Divinity*, 561–77. La Salle, Ill.

GASKIN, J. C. A. 'David Hume and the Eighteenth-Century Interest in Miracles', *Hermathena* no. 99, 80–92.

GASKIN, J. C. A. *The arguments and opinions of David Hume concerning religion and the being and attributes of God*. Oxford U. (diss.).

HARRÉ, H. R. 'Concepts and Criteria', *Mind* 73, 353–63.

HAYMOND, W. S. 'Hume's Phenomenalism', *Mod. Schoolman* 41, 209–26.

HUDSON, W. D. 'Hume on *Is* and *Ought*', *Phil. Q.* 14, 246–52, (on MacIntyre 1959 and Hunter 1962). (repr. 1966 in Chappell, *Hume*; 1969 in Hudson, *The Is-Ought Question*)

JEFFNER, A. 'Humes definition av god', *Svensk Teologisk Kvartalsskrift* 40, 203–12.

KEMP, J. *Reason, Action and Morality*, ch. 4. London.

LÖWISCH, D. J. *Immanuel Kant und David Humes 'Dialogues concerning Natural Religion' : ein Versuch zur Aufhellung der Bedeutung von Humes Spätschrift für die Philosophie Immanuel Kants, im besonderen für die 'Kritik der reinen Vernunft'*. Bonn.

MANDELBAUM, M. *Philosophy, Science, and Sense Perception*, Essay 3, '"Of Scepticism with Regard to the Senses"', 118–70. Baltimore. [*P* 40 (1965) 264–6]

MATCZAK, S. A. 'A Select and Classified Bibliography of David Hume', *Mod. Schoolman* 42, 70–81.

MATTHEWS, G. 'Theology and Natural Theology', *J. Phil.* 61, 99–108. (repr. 1973 in W. L. Rowe & W. J. Wainwright, *Philosophy of Religion*)

MOLINARI, E. 'Stato di diritto e Stato di giustizia in Hume', *Riv. int. Fil. Diritto* 41, 243–8.

MOLINARI, E. *L'utopia controllata, Considerazioni sulla filosofia morale di D. Hume*. (157 pp.) Milan.

NELSON, J. O. 'The Conclusion of Book One, Part Four of Hume's *Treatise*', *Phil. & phenomenol. Res.* 24, 512–21.

NOXON, J. 'Hume's Agnosticism', *Phil. Rev.* 73, 248–61. (repr. 1966 in Chappell, *Hume*) [*JHP* 14 (1976) 301–11; 469–73]

OBIDNIAK, E. 'Hume'a teoria percepcji a jego stanowisko gnoseologiczne', *Acta Universitatis Wratislaviensis* 21, 103–34.

PASSELL, D. *Hume on probability*. Stanford U. (diss.).

PETROVIĆ, G. *Od Loka do Ejera* (From Locke to Ayer). Zagreb.

POPKIN, R. H. 'So, Hume Did Read Berkeley', *J. Phil.* 61, 773–8. (on Wiener 1961) [*P* 43 (1968) 278–80]

PRICE, J. V. 'Sceptics in Cicero and Hume', *J. Hist. Ideas* 25, 97–106.

RAYNOR, O. 'Hume's Scepticism Regarding "Probable Reasoning" in the *Treatise*', *Sth. J. Phil.* 2, 103–6.

SCHEFFLER, J. *The Anatomy of Inquiry*, pt. 3, sec. 2, 'Hume's Challenge and the Generalization Formula' (227–36). London.

SMART, N. *Philosophers and Religious Truth*, ch. 2 ('Miracles and David Hume'). London.

SWEIGART, J. 'The Distance between Hume and Emotivism', *Phil. Q.* 14, 229–36. [*P St* (Irel.) 19 (1970) 202–13]

TANAKA, T. 'Economist to shite no David Hume' (Hume as an economist), *Keizaigaku Ronkyū* 18, no. 1.

TANAKA, T. 'Hume no *Political Discourses* o meguru keizaigaku ronso ni tsuite' (The economic controversies in connection with Hume's *Political Discourses*), *Keizaigaku Ronkyū* 18, no. 2.

TANAKA, T. 'Hyūmu ni okeru sozei to keizai' (Taxation and economy in David Hume), *Keizaigaku Ronkyū* 18, 399–418.

TANAKA, T. 'David Hume as an Economist', *Kwansei Gakuin Univ. Annual Studies* 13, 113–29.

TOVO, J. C. *The experience of causal efficacy in Whitehead and Hume.* Indiana U. (diss.).

WAWRZYNIAK, A. 'Koncepcja stosunku przyczynowego według Dawida Hume'a', *Roczniki filozoficzne* 12, 39–51.

WEINBERG, J. R. 'The Novelty of Hume's Philosophy', *Proc. Am. phil. Ass.* 38, 17–35.

WILBANKS, J. J. *Hume's theory of imagination.* Ohio State U. (diss.).

WILLEY, B. *The English Moralists*, ch. 16. London.

WILLIAMS, R. 'David Hume: Reasoning and Experience', in H. S. Davies & G. Watson, *The English Mind*, ch. 7. Cambridge.

YOUNG, T. A. *Change in Aristotle, Descartes, Hume and Whitehead.* Indiana U. (diss.).

ZABEEH, F. 'Hume on Pure and Applied Geometry', *Ratio* 6, 185–91. [*Ratio* 8 (1966) 96–100]

[1965]

BARRY, B. *Political Argument*, 319–21. London.

BELGION, M. *David Hume.* (Br. Council, Writers and their Work, no. 181) London.

BENN, T. V. 'Les *Political discourses* de David Hume et un conte de Diderot', in *Currents of Thought in French Literature: Essays in memory of G. T. Clapton*, 253–76. Oxford.

BONGIE, L. L. *David Hume, Prophet of the Counter-revolution.* Oxford.
[*TLS* (7 July 1966) 593; *Am. hist. Rev.* 72 (1966) 201–2; *Hermathena* no. 104 (1967) 83–5; *JHP* 5 (1967) 370–2; *P* 43 (1968) 179–80]

BRUNET, O. *Philosophie et esthétique chez David Hume.* (955 pp.) Paris. [*PQ* 17 (1967) 378–80]

CAIN, R. E. 'David Hume and Adam Smith as sources of the concept of sympathy in Hazlitt', *Papers in Engl. Lang. & Lit.*, 1 133–40.

CAPALDI, N. *The philosophy of David Hume.* (Monarch notes and study guides) New York.

CAPALDI, N. *Judgment and sentiment in Hume's moral theory.* Columbia U. (diss.).

COHEN, R. *Essential Works of David Hume.* New York. (anthol.)

DAY, John. 'Hume on Justice and Allegiance', *Philosophy* 40, 35–56.

DOBSON, P. G. *David Hume's theory of history, a study of the relationship between his philosophical, sociological, and historical methodology.* New York U. (diss.).

EDGLEY, R. 'Practical Reason', *Mind* 74, 174–91.

FLEMING, B. N. 'The Idea of a Solid', *Australas. J. Phil.* 43, 131–43.

GARNETT, A. C. *The Perceptual Process*, 86–91. Madison.

GEORGE, R. J. *The role of points in Hume's analysis of space.* U. of Notre Dame (diss.).

GRIMSLEY, R. & RONCO, D. D. 'Corrispondenti italiani di David Hume', *Riv. crit. Stor. Fil.* 20, 407–13.

HARRISON, W. *Conflict and Compromise: History of British Political Thought, 1593–1900*, 93–101. New York & London.

HEARN, T. K. *The objectivism of Hume's ethics.* Vanderbilt U. (diss.).

HILL, R. S. *The political philosophy of David Hume.* U. of Chicago (diss.).

HOLLAND, R. F. 'The Miraculous', *Am. phil. Q.* 2, 43–51. (repr. 1972 in J. Donnelly, *Logical Analysis and Contemporary Theism*) [*PQ* 26 (1976) 69–81]

HUNTER, G. B. B. 'A Possible Extension of Logical Theory ?', *Phil. Studies* 16, 81–8.

HURLBUTT, R. H. *Hume, Newton, and the Design Argument.* Lincoln, Neb.
[*JP* 63 (1966) 161–6; *P* 41 (1966) 181–2; *M* 76 (1967) 456]

KING, E. G. *The concept of spiritual substance in the empiricist philosophy of George Berkeley.* U. of Notre Dame (diss.).

LANGLEY, R. J. *Hume's logic of the imagination.* Fordham U. (diss.).

LENZ, J. W. *David Hume, Of the Standard of Taste, and Other Essays.* Indianapolis.
[*RM* 19 (1965–6) 813; *JHP* 5 (1967) 311–12; *MS* 46 (1968–9) 379]

LETWIN, S. R. *The Pursuit of Certainty*, pt. 1. Cambridge.

McGUINNESS, A. E. *The influence of David Hume's critical theory on Lord Kames's 'Elements of Criticism'.* U. of Wisconsin (diss.).

MACINTYRE, A.C. *Hume's Ethical Writings*. New York.
(anthol.) (*Enquiry, A Dialogue, Treatise* II.iii.3 and sections of
III, three *Essays*, and *Dialogues* pts. X–XI)

MEEROVSKI, B.V. Article (in Russian) on Hume and
Charles de Brosses, in *Filosofskie Nauki* 6, 79–84.

MILLER, E.F. *The political philosophy of David Hume: an
interpretation of its mode*. U. of Chicago (diss.).

MOSSNER, E.C. 'The Enlightenment of David Hume', in
R. Mollenauer, *Introduction to Modernity*, 43–62. Austin,
Texas. (repr. 1967: see Mossner 1967)

NORTON, D.F. 'History and Philosophy in Hume's Thought',
in the following, pp. xxxii–l.

NORTON, D.F. & POPKIN, R.H. *David Hume: Philosophical
Historian*. Indianapolis. (anthol.) [*JHP* 6 (1968) 105]

NUCHELMANS, G. *David Hume*. Baarn.
[*Dialoog* 6 (1965–6) 250–1]

PASHMAN, J. 'Baier on Hume', *Sth. J. Phil*. 2, 127–30.
(on Baier 1958)

POUMIER, H. 'Hume et le problème de la liberté',
Études phil. 20, 37–46.

PRICE, J.V. *The Ironic Hume*. Austin, Texas.
[*Études anglaises* 19 (1965) 192; *JHP* 5 (1967) 94]

RICHARDS, T.J. 'Hume's Two Definitions of "Cause"',
Phil. Q. 15, 247–53. (on Robinson 1962) (repr. 1966 in
Chappell, *Hume*; with Robinson's reply, 162–8)

SABETTI, A. *David Hume, filosofo della religione*. (183 pp.)
Naples.
[*G. di Metafisica* 21 (1966) 875–6; *RCSF* 21 (1966) 345]

SANTUCCI, A. 'Hume e i "philosophes"', *Riv. Fil*. 56, 150–77.
(repr. 1965 in his *L'Umanesimo scettico . . .*)

SANTUCCI, A. 'Problemi e orientamenti della critica humiana',
Riv. crit. Stor. Fil. 20, 313–35. (repr. 1966 in *Studi sull'
Illuminismo*, 47–69, Florence)

SANTUCCI, A. *L'Umanesimo scettico di David Hume*. Bologna.

SEMMEL, B. 'The Hume-Tucker Debate and Pitt's Trade
Proposals', *Econ. J*. 75, 759–70.

SESONSKE, A. & FLEMING, N. *Human Understanding: Studies
in the Philosophy of David Hume*. Belmont, Calif. (contains
reprints of Price 1940, Penelhum 1955, Flew 1961, pp. 19–50;
and C.D. Broad, 'Hume's Theory of the Credibility of
Miracles', from *Proc. Arist. Soc*. 17 [1916/17] 77–94)

STOVE, D. 'Hume, Probability, and Induction', *Phil. Rev*. 74,
160–77. (repr. 1966 in Chappell, *Hume*; 1970 in J.H. Gill,
Philosophy Today 3, New York)

TANAKA, T. 'David Hume no Kōsai ron' (David Hume on the public debt), *Keizaigaku Ronkyū* 19, 33–58.

TAYLOR, W.L. *Francis Hutcheson and David Hume as predecessors of Adam Smith*, passim. Durham, N.C.

TREVOR-ROPER, H.R. 'Three Historians—11: David Hume', *Listener* 74, 521–4.

VINER, J. 'Guide to John Rae's *Life of Adam Smith*', esp. 49–58 (introduction to 1965 reprint of Rae, *Life of Adam Smith*, in the series Reprints of Economic Classics). New York.

WEINBERG, J.R. *Abstraction, Relation, and Induction*, 32–41. Madison & Milwaukee.

WILLIAMS, M.E. 'Kant's Reply to Hume', *Kant-Studien* 56, 71–8. (on Schipper 1961) [*Ratio* 9 (1967) 33–7]

[1966]

ANDERSON, R.F. *Hume's First Principles*. Lincoln, Neb. [*PQ* 17 (1967) 285; *JHP* 6 (1968) 88–91]

ÁRDAL, P.S. *Passion and Value in Hume's Treatise*. Edinburgh. [*JHP* 5 (1967) 372–3; *P* 43 (1968) 177–9; *M* 77 (1968) 614–15; *JP* 65 (1968) 257–60; *PQ* 18 (1968) 83–4; *PR* 78 (1969) 127–9; *D* 8 (1969/70) 692–7; *P* 48 (1973) 288–92]

BARBER, K.F. *Meinong's 'Hume Studies'; translation and commentary*. U. of Iowa (diss.).

BEARDSLEY, M.C. *Aesthetics from Classical Greece to the Present: A short history*, 187–91. New York & London. [*PR* 78 (1969) 272–3]

BEITZINGER, A.J. 'Hume's Aristocratic Preference', *Rev. Polit.* 28, 154–71.

BENNETT, J.F. *Kant's Analytic*, esp. secs. 38–9 ('Kant and Hume on causality' and 'Necessity and universality'). Cambridge.

CAPALDI, N. 'Hume's Rejection of "Ought" as a Moral Category', *J. Phil.* 63, 126–37. (repr. 1975, with minor revisions, in ch.7 of his *David Hume*) [*JP* 64 (1967) 451–3]

CAPALDI, N. 'Some Misconceptions about Hume's Moral Theory', *Ethics* 76, 208–11.

CAPITAN, W.H. 'Part X of Hume's *Dialogues*', *Am. phil. Q.* 3, 82–5. (repr. 1966 in Chappell, *Hume*)

CHAPPELL, V.C. *Hume: A collection of critical essays*. New York. (publ. London & Melbourne 1968) (repr. 1968, Notre Dame, Ind.) (contains Flew, Nathan, Robinson— see below; and reprints Mossner 1950, Popkin 1951,

Jessop 1952, Penelhum 1955, Wand 1956, Lenz 1958,
MacIntyre 1959, Wolff 1960, Atkinson 1961, Robinson 1962,
Flew 1963, Hayek 1963, Hunter 1963, Hudson 1964,
Noxon 1964, Richards 1965, Stove 1965, Capitan 1966)
[*RM* 20 (1966) 555–6]

CZARNECKI, Z. 'Dawid Hume (1711–1776) jako krytyk religii'
(Article in Polish on Hume's criticism of religion),
Euhemer 10, 55–69.

DAVID, M. 'Lettres inédites de Diderot et de Hume écrites de
1755 à 1763 au Président de Brosses', *Revue phil.* 91, 135–44.

DUCASSE, C. J. 'Critique of Hume's Conception of Causality',
J. Phil. 63, 141–8. (repr. 1974 in T. L. Beauchamp,
Philosophical Problems of Causation, Encino & Belmont)

ENGEL, C.-E. '1776-un duel à la mort: Rousseau et Hume',
Nouvelles Littéraires, 4 Aug.

FLEW, A. ' "Not Proven" — At Most', in V. C. Chappell, *Hume*,
291–4. New York. (on Hunter 1963)

FLEW, A. 'Did Hume Distinguish Pure from Applied
Geometry ?', *Ratio* 8, 96–100. (on Zabeeh 1964)

FOSTER, L. *Hume's theory of moral judgments*. U. of Pennsylvania
(diss.).

GAY, P. *The Enlightenment: An Interpretation*, vol. 1, ch. 7, sec. 3
(401–19). New York. (publ. London 1967) (For vol. 2, see
1970)

GRENE, M. *The Knower and the Known*, ch. 4. London.
(revision of Grene 1955)

HARRIS, M. H. 'David Hume: Scholar as Librarian',
Libr. Q. 36, 88–98.

HICK, J. *Evil and the God of Love*, 338–45 and 360–7. London.
(2nd edn 1977)

HILL, K. C. *Interpreting Literature*, ch. 4 (99–150: 'Philosophy').
Chicago & London. (literary study of the second *Inquiry*)

JACOBSON, N. P. 'Gotama Buddha et David Hume',
Revue phil. 91, 145–63.

JACOBSON, N. P. *Buddhism: The Religion of Analysis*, ch. 8.
London.

JEFFNER, A. *Butler and Hume on Religion: A comparative
analysis*. Stockholm. [*PR* 77 (1968) 369–72]

JORDAN, J. N. *Hume's account of the conception of physical
objects*. U. of Texas (diss.).

KOŁAKOWSKI, L. *Filozofia Pozytywistyczna*, ch. 2. Warsaw.
(transl. 1968 as *The Alienation of Reason: A History of
Positivist Thought*, New York; repr. 1972 as *Positivist
Philosophy: From Hume to the Vienna Circle*, Harmondsworth)

LÖWISCH, D.-J. 'Kants *Kritik der reinen Vernunft* und Humes *Dialogues* . . .', *Kant-Studien* 56, 170–207.

MELDEN, A.I. 'Desires as Causes of Actions', in F.C. Dommeyer, *Current Philosophical Issues: Essays in honor of Curt John Ducasse*, 127–50. Springfield, Ill.

MORRISROE, M. *The rhetoric of the Dialogues of David Hume.* U. of Texas (diss.).

MURPHY, J.S. 'Hume's Analogies in *Treatise* I and the Commentators', *J. Hist. Phil.* 4, 155–9.

NATHAN, G.J. 'Hume's Immanent God', in V.C. Chappell, *Hume*, 396–423. New York.
    [*RS* 11 (1975) 19–35; *Phil. Papers* 5 (1976) 121–34]

NEILL, W.H.D. 'Some Attacks on Causality prior to Hume', *Vivarium* 4, 58–65.

NELSON, J.O. 'Tastes', *Phil. & phenomenol. Res.* 26, 537–45.

NORTON, D.F. *From moral sense to common sense: an essay on the development of Scottish common sense philosophy, 1700–1765.* U. of Calif., San Diego (diss.).

PALUCH, S. 'Hume and the Miraculous', *Dialogue* 5, 61–5.

PAUL, R. 'Appearances and Expectations', *J. Phil.* 63, 585. (abstract of Paul 1969)

PRICE, J.V. 'Hume's Concept of Liberty and *The History of England*', *Studies in Romanticism* 5, 139–57.

ROBINSON, J.A. 'Hume's Two Definitions of "Cause" Reconsidered', in V.C. Chappell, *Hume*, 162–8. New York. (on Richards 1965) [*Personalist* 56 (1975) 361–2]

ROSS, I. 'Hutcheson on Hume's *Treatise*: An Unnoticed Letter', *J. Hist. Phil.* 4, 69–72.

STRAWSON, P.F. *The Bounds of Sense*, pt. 3, ch. 2, sec. 3 ('Hume and Kant on the self'). London.

SUCHTING, W.A. 'Hume and Necessary Truth', *Dialogue* 5, 47–60.

WINNETT, A.R. 'Johnson and Hume', *New Rambler* 1, 2–14.

[1967]

BECK, L.W. 'Kant's Strategy', *J. Hist. Ideas* 28, 224–36.

BECK, L.W. 'Once More Unto the Breach: Kant's Answer to Hume, Again', *Ratio* 9, 33–7. [11 (1969) 75–87] (all repr. 1974 in T.L. Beauchamp, *Philosophical Problems of Causation*, Encino & Belmont)

BRAUDY, L.B. *The narrative stance: problems on history and methods of fiction in David Hume, Henry Fielding, and Edward Gibbon.* Yale U. (diss.). (cf. Braudy 1970)

CAMPBELL, R. L. *An examination of David Hume's philosophy of determinism.* U. of Utah (diss.).

CLARK, L. W. *The moral and political philosophy of David Hume.* Yale U. (diss.).

COLLINS, J. D. *The British Empiricists: Locke, Berkeley, Hume.* Milwaukee. (anthol.)

COLLINS, J. *The Emergence of Philosophy of Religion,* chs. 1–2. New Haven & London.

CORSANO, A. 'Hume e il teatro', *Belfagor* 22, 81–5.

COSTA, M. 'Acerca de la importancia histórica de Hume', *Rev. Fil.* (La Plata) 19, 85–94.

DAL PRA, M. 'L'astrazione nella filosofia di Hume', *Riv. crit. Stor. Fil.* 22, 435–56. (repr. 1968 in Leroy, *Studi su Hume*)

DAVIDSON, D. 'Causal Relations', *J. Phil.* 64, 691–703. (repr. 1974 in T. L. Beauchamp, *Philosophical Problems of Causation,* Encino & Belmont)

DAVIE, G. E. 'Hume, Reid, and the passion for ideas', in G. Bruce, *Edinburgh in the Age of Reason,* 23–39. Edinburgh.

DENIS, H. *Histoire de la pensée économique,* 153–9. Paris.

DESJARDINS, G. 'Terms of *De Officiis* in Hume and Kant', *J. Hist. Ideas* 28, 237–42.

FLEW, A. 'Infinite Divisibility in Hume's *Treatise*', *Riv. crit. Stor. Fil.* 22, 457–71. (repr. 1968 in Leroy, *Studi su Hume*; 1976 in Livingston & King, *Hume: A Re-evaluation*)

FLEW, A. 'Miracles', in P. Edwards, *The Encyclopedia of Philosophy* (vol. 5, 346–53). New York.

FURLEY, D. J. *Two Studies in the Greek Atomists,* Study 1, ch. 10 ('Epicurus and David Hume'). Princeton.

GLOSSOP, R. J. 'The Nature of Hume's Ethics', *Phil. & phenomenol. Res.* 27, 527–36. (repr. 1970 in J. H. Gill, *Philosophy Today* 3, New York)

GLOSSOP, R. J. 'Hume's Rejection of "Ought"', *J. Phil.* 64, 451–3. (on Capaldi 1966)

GUGGENHEIM, T. 'L'idée de neutralité monétaire chez David Hume', *Revue écon. et soc.* 25, 309–18.

HALL, R. 'Did Hume Read Some Berkeley Unawares ?', *Philosophy* 42, 276–7.

HAUSMAN, A. 'Hume's Theory of Relations', *Noûs* 1, 255–82.

HAZO, R. G. *The Idea of Love,* 441–7. New York.

HELM, P. 'Hume on Exculpation', *Philosophy* 42, 265–71.

JESSOP, T. E. 'Hume: Philosopher or psychologist ? A problem of Exegesis', *Riv. crit. Stor. Fil.* 22, 418–34. (repr. 1968 in Leroy, *Studi su Hume*)

KAMPF, L. See 1971.

KING, J. T., JR. *The development of Hume's moral philosophy from 1740 to 1751: the relationship of the 'Treatise' and the second 'Inquiry'*. U. of Notre Dame (diss.).

KIVY, P. 'Hume's Standard of Taste: Breaking the Circle', *Br. J. Aesth.* 7, 57–66.

LEROY, A.-L. 'Le rôle de David Hume dans la philosophie moderne', *Riv. crit. Stor. Fil.* 22, 371–87. (repr. 1968 in Leroy, *Studi su Hume*)

LUDASSY, M. 'Az ujkori angol filozófusok a vallásról. 11: Locke és Hume' (English philosophers on religion in modern times—Locke and Hume), *Világosság* 8, 659–65.

MACINTYRE, A. C. *A Short History of Ethics*, 168–77. London.

MACNABB, D. G. C. 'Hume, David', in P. Edwards, *The Encyclopedia of Philosophy* (vol. 4, 74–90). New York.

MALL, R. A. *Hume's Concept of Man: An essay in philosophical anthropology*. Bombay. (cf. Mall 1963)

MERLAN, P. 'Kant, Hamann-Jacobi and Schelling on Hume', *Riv. crit. Stor. Fil.* 22, 481–94. (repr. 1968 in Leroy, *Studi su Hume*; 1976 in Merlan, *Kleine Philosophische Schriften*, Hildesheim & New York)

MIGLIORINI, E. 'Nota a "La regola del gusto"', *Riv. crit. Stor. Fil.* 22, 472–80. (repr. 1968 in Leroy, *Studi su Hume*)

MOSSNER, E. C. 'Hume's "Of Criticism"', in H. Anderson & J. S. Shea, *Studies in Criticism and Aesthetics, 1660–1800: Essays in honor of Samuel Holt Monk*, 232–48. Minneapolis.

MOSSNER, E. C. 'The Enlightenment of David Hume', *Riv. crit. Stor. Fil.* 22, 388–99. (repr. of 1965 article; repr. 1968 in Leroy, *Studi su Hume*)

MOSSNER, E. C. & PRICE, J. V. *David Hume, A Letter from a Gentleman to his friend in Edinburgh* (1745). Edinburgh. (French transl. by D. Deleule, with facing original, Paris 1977) [*JHP* 6 (1968) 161–7]

NARSKY, I. S. Философия Давида Юма. (355 pp.) Moscow. [*Mind* 78 (1969) 311–13]

OSBORNE, H. 'Hume's Standard and the Diversity of Aesthetic Taste', *Br. J. Aesth.* 7, 50–6.

PEARS, D. F. *Bertrand Russell and the British Tradition in Philosophy*, ch. 2 ('Hume's System'). London.

PENELHUM, T. The section on Hume of 'Personal Identity', in P. Edwards, *The Encyclopedia of Philosophy* (vol. 6, 98–100). New York.

PENNINO, L. 'Sul problema della causalità in Hume e Kant', *Filosofia e Vita* 8, 39–43.

PIKE, N. 'Hume's Bundle Theory of the Self: A Limited Defence', *Am. phil. Q.* 4, 159–65.

PLANTINGA, A. *God and Other Minds*, ch. 4 ('The Teleological Argument'). Ithaca & London.

POPKIN, R. H. 'Hume and Jurieu: possible Calvinist origins of Hume's Theory of Belief', *Riv. crit. Stor. Fil.* 22, 400–17. (repr. 1968 in Leroy, *Studi su Hume*)

POPKIN, R. H. 'Skepticism', in P. Edwards, *The Encyclopedia of Philosophy* (vol. 7, 449–61, esp. 455–7). New York.

POTTLE, F. A. 'The Part Played by Horace Walpole and James Boswell in the Quarrel between Rousseau and Hume: A Reconsideration', in Warren Hunting Smith, *Horace Walpole*, 255–91. New Haven.

PRICE, J. V. 'Concepts of enlightenment in 18th-century Scottish literature', *Texas Studies in Lit. & Lang.* 9, 371–9.

RONCHETTI, E. 'Bibliografia humiana dal 1937 al 1966', *Riv. crit. Stor. Fil.* 22, 495–520. (repr. 1968 in Leroy, *Studi su Hume*)

SOVERAL, E. A. DE. 'O problema das Influências de Locke e de Hume em Kant', *Rev. portuguesa de fil.* 23, 161–83.

SPRAGUE, E. 'Moral Sense', in P. Edwards, *The Encyclopedia of Philosophy* (vol. 5, 385–7). New York.

STEGMÜLLER, F. 'Towards a Rational Reconstruction of Kant's Metaphysics of Experience', pt. 1, *Ratio* 9, 1–32.

STONE, R. V. *Hume's rationalism*. U. of Texas, Austin (diss.).

SWAIN, C. W. 'Hamann and the Philosophy of David Hume', *J. Hist. Phil.* 5, 343–51.

TAYLOR, R. 'Causation', in P. Edwards, *The Encyclopedia of Philosophy* (vol. 2, 56–66). New York.

WILKINS, B. T. *The Problem of Burke's Political Philosophy*, esp. 50–71. Oxford.

WOOZLEY, A. D. 'Universals', in P. Edwards, *The Encyclopedia of Philosophy* (vol. 8, 194–206, esp. 202–3). New York.

WORLEY, J. H. *Hume's theory of ideas*. Northwestern U. (diss.).

[1968]

AYERS, M. R. *The Refutation of Determinism*, esp. ch. 4. London.

BRISSENDEN, R. F. '"Sentiment": Some Uses of the Word in the Writings of David Hume', in Brissenden, *Studies in the Eighteenth Century*, 89–107. Canberra.

CAPALDI, N. 'Reid's Critique of Hume's Moral Theory', *Phil. J.* 5, 43–6.

CARABELLI, G. 'L'alibi strutturale di Hume nei *Dialogues . . .*', *Strumenti critici* 2, 87–110.

CAVENDISH, A. P. *David Hume.* New York. (repr. of Basson 1958)

COLE, R. 'The Logical Order and the Causal Order', in P. G. Kuntz, *The Concept of Order*, 111–21. Seattle & London.

COOK, J. W. 'Hume's Scepticism with Regard to the Senses', *Am. phil. Q.* 5, 1–17.

COOK, T. I. 'Reflections On The Moral and Political Philosophy of David Hume: A Review Article', *Studies in Burke and His Time* (formerly *The Burke Newsletter*) 9, 949–58. (on Stewart 1963)

COWLEY, F. *A Critique of British Empiricism*, esp. chs. 1–11 (1–105). London, etc. [*D* 7 (1968) 491–4]

CRANSTON, M. *Political Dialogues*, ch. 4 ('A Dialogue on Morality, between Voltaire and David Hume'). London.

CZARNECKI, Z. 'Dawid Hume w oczach swoich współczesnych', *Ruch Filozoficzny* no. 43, 339–41.

DIETL, P. 'Hume on the Passions', *Phil. & phenomenol. Res.* 28, 554–66.

GASKIN, J. C. A. 'Hume's suppressed dissertations: an authentic text', *Hermathena* no. 106, 54–9.

GAWLICK, G. *David Hume, Dialoge über natürliche Religion*, neu bearbeitet. Hamburg. (Paulsen translation, revised, with introduction)

HALL, R. 'Hume's Actual Use of Berkeley's *Principles*', *Philosophy* 43, 278–80.
[*P* 44 (1969) 238–42; 45 (1970) 152–3]

HALL, R. 'Unnoticed Words in Hume and Others', *Notes & Queries* 213, 445–8.

HUFF, T. P. *Hume on moral obligation.* Rice U. (diss.).

KIMMEL, L. D. *A critical appraisal of the moral philosophy of David Hume.* U. of Texas (diss.).

LEROY, A.-L. et al. *Studi su Hume.* Florence. (reprints [all 1967] Leroy, Mossner ['The Enlightenment . . .'], Popkin, Jessop, Dal Pra, Flew, Migliorini, Merlan, and Ronchetti)

McCLENNAN, E. F. *Justice as an object of rational decision.* Johns Hopkins U. (diss.).

MATHEWS, B. R. *Hume's theory of sympathy.* Johns Hopkins U. (diss.).

MATSON, W. I. *A History of Philosophy*, 365–90. New York, etc.

MAXWELL, N. 'Can there be Necessary Connections between Successive Events ?', *Br. J. Phil. Sci.* 19, 1–25. (repr. 1974 in R. Swinburne, *The Justification of Induction*, Oxford)

MENZEL, L. 'Kant und Hume', *Sborník Prací Filosofické Fakulty Brněnské University* 17, 25–37.

MICHAEL, S. J. *An examination of the role of natural belief in David Hume's philosophy of religion.* Harvard U. (diss.).

MYERS, R. E. *Studies in method and religion in Hume's 'Science of Human Nature'.* Ohio State U. (diss.).

NORTON, D. F. 'Hume's *A Letter From a Gentleman*, A Review Note', *J. Hist. Phil.* 6, 161–7.

OLSEN, S. H. 'Perspsjoner, inntrykk, ideer og objekter i Bok I, Del I av Humes Treatise' (Perceptions, impressions, ideas and objects in Book I, Part I of Hume's Treatise). *Norsk Filosofisk Tidsskrift* 3, 221–8.

OPPENHEIM, F. E. *Moral Principles in Political Philosophy,* 151–9. New York.

PETRELLA, F. 'Adam Smith's Rejection of Hume's Price-Specie-Flow Mechanism: A Minor Mystery Resolved', *Sth. econ. J.* 34, 365–74.

PORTER, B. F. *Deity and Morality,* ch. 2. London.

PRICE, J. V. *David Hume.* (174 pp.) (Twayne English Authors) New York.

RING, B. A. 'David Hume: Historian or Tory Hack?', *North Dakota Q.* 36, 50–9.

ROTENSTREICH, N. 'On the Position of Maimon's Philosophy', *Rev. Met.* 21, 534–45.

ROTWEIN, E. 'Hume, David', in D. L. Sills, *International Encyclopedia of the Social Sciences* (vol. 6, 546–50).

SOKOLOWSKI, R. 'Fiction and Illusion in David Hume's Philosophy', *Mod. Schoolman* 45, 189–225.

STOCKTON, C. N. *David Hume's constitutional history of England.* Claremont Grad. Sch. (diss.).

SWINBURNE, R. G. 'The Argument from Design', *Philosophy* 43, 199–212. (repr. 1972 in J. Donnelly, *Logical Analysis & Contemporary Theism*; 1974 in B. Brody, *Readings in the Philosophy of Religion*, Englewood Cliffs, N.J.) [*RS* 12 (1976) 331–45; *Analysis* 37 (1977) 113–16]

SWINBURNE, R. G. 'Miracles', *Phil. Q.* 18, 320–8. (repr. 1973 in W. L. Rowe & W. J. Wainwright, *Philosophy of Religion*)

TANAKA, T. 'Hume no *History of England* no Ichi Kosatsu' (Re-evaluation of Hume's *History of England*), *Keizaigaku Ronkyū* 21, no. 4.

VITIELLO, V. '"Feeling" e "Relation" nella filosofia del conoscere di D. Hume', *Atti dell' Accad. di Scienze morali* 79. Naples.

WATKINS, J.W.N. 'Hume, Carnap and Popper', in
   I. Lakatos, *The Problem of Inductive Logic*, 271–82.
   Amsterdam.
WILBANKS, J. *Hume's Theory of Imagination*. The Hague.
   [*Stromata* 25 (1969) 447–8]
WOOD, R.A. *An inquiry into the 'Treatise'*. U. of Nebraska
   (diss.).

[1969]

BARONCELLI, F. 'Hume tra sistema e ricerca', *Ethica* 8, 141–5.
BECK, L.W. 'Lambert und Hume in Kants Entwicklung von
   1769–1772', *Kant-Studien* 60, 123–30.
BITZER, L.F. 'Hume's Philosophy in George Campbell's
   Philosophy of Rhetoric', *Phil. & Rhetoric* 2, 139–66.
BRITTON, K. *Philosophy and the Meaning of Life*, ch. 5.
   Cambridge.
BUCHDAHL, G. *Metaphysics and the Philosophy of Science*,
   ch. 6 ('Hume: The Critique of Causation'). Oxford.
CAPPIELLO, I. *Hume, critico della ragione*. (158 pp.) Naples.
CARRIVE, P. 'Passion, convention et institution dans la pensée
   de Hume', *Étud. phil.* 24, 371–81.
CASTIGNONE, S. 'Il Problema del Rapporto tra "Is" e "Ought".
   Saggio de bibliografia ragionata con riferimento al pensiero
   di David Hume, 1959–1967', *Annali della Facoltà di
   Giurisprudenza della Univ. de Genova* 8, 239–61.
CHISHOLM, R.M. 'On the Observability of the Self',
   Phil. & phenomenol. Res. 30, 7–21. (repr. 1972 in J. Donnelly,
   Logical Analysis & Contemporary Theism; main part repr.
   1976 in Chisholm, *Person and Object*, as sec. 6 of ch. 1)
   [33 (1972–73) 338–49; *PSt* 26 (1974) 69–71;
   J. crit. Anal. 6 (1975) 13–21]
COHEN, M.F. 'The Practicality of Moral Reasoning', *Mind* 78,
   534–49.
CONROY, G.P. 'Did Hume Really Follow Berkeley ?',
   Philosophy 44, 238–42. (on Hall 1968)
   [45 (1970) 152–3]
CREEL, R.E. 'The Is-Ought Controversy', *Kinesis* 1, 107–20.
CUNNINGHAM, G.W. 'On Reason's Reach: Historical
   Observations', *Am. phil. Q.* 6, 1–16.
DOHERTY, F. 'Sterne and Hume: A Bicentenary Essay',
   Essays & Studies 22, 71–87.
EDGLEY, R. *Reason in Theory and Practice*, ch. 1. London.
GLIDDEN, J.C. *Hume on superstition*. U. of Colorado (diss.).

HARRIS, E. E. *Fundamentals of Philosophy*, chs. 24–6. London.

HARTNACK, J. *Filosofiens Historie*, 138–54. Copenhagen.

HEARN, T. K. 'Norman Kemp Smith on "Natural Belief"',
Sth. J. Phil. 7, 3–7.

HENZE, D. F. 'The Linguistic Aspect of Hume's Method',
J. Hist. Ideas 30, 116–26.

HUDSON, W. D. *The Is-Ought Question*. London. (includes
MacIntyre 1959, Atkinson 1961, Hunter 1962, Flew 1963,
Hunter 1963, Hudson 1964)

JACOBSON, N. P. 'The Possibility of Oriental Influence in
Hume's Philosophy', *Phil. East & West* 19, 17–37.
[*Int. phil. Q.* 17 (1977) 135–46]

JUFFRAS, A. *Hume's theory of meaning*. Columbia U. (diss.).

KAUFMANN, W. 'The Origin of Justice', *Rev. Met.* 23, 203–39.

KEKES, J. 'Beliefs and Scepticism', *Phil. Forum* 1, 353–8.

KENNY, A. *The Five Ways*, 66–8. London.
[*PR* 80 (1971) 414–15]

LAUENER, H. *Hume und Kant: eine systematische
Gegenüberstellung einiger Hauptpunkte ihrer Lehren*. (228 pp.)
Berne & Munich.
[*Biblio. of Phil.* 17 (1970) 438–9; *KS* 62 (1971) 252–3;
Schweizer Monatshefte 52 (1972/3) 131–7]

LIVINGSTON, D. W. *A study of the idea of history in Hume's
metaphysics*. Washington U. (diss.).

LONGLEY, P. M. *Hume's logic: ideas and inference*.
U. of Minnesota (diss.).

McGUINNESS, A. E. 'Hume and Kames: The Burden of
Friendship', *Studies in Scott. Lit.* (U. of S. Carolina) 6,
3–19. [186–9]

MADDEN, E. H. 'A Third View of Causality', *Rev. Met.* 23,
67–84. (repr. 1974 in T. L. Beauchamp,
Philosophical Problems of Causation, Encino & Belmont)

MORRISROE, M. 'Hume's Rhetorical Strategy: A Solution to
the Riddle of the *Dialogues* . . .', *Texas Studies in Lit. & Lang.*
11, 963–74.

MORRISROE, M. 'Rhetorical Methods in Hume's Works on
Religion', *Phil. & Rhetoric* 2, 121–38.

MOSSNER, E. C. *David Hume, A Treatise of Human Nature*.
(repr. of 1st edn, with Hume's corrections; more are now
known: see Connon 1975) Harmondsworth.
[For corrections of this edition, see Nidditch 1976]

MURPHY, J. G. 'Kant's Second Analogy as an Answer to Hume',
Ratio 11, 75–8. (on Beck 1967) [82–7]

OTTEN, T. 'A Borrowing from Hume', *Notes & Queries* 214 (16), 189–90.

PAUL, Robt. 'Appearances and Expectations', *Mind* 78, 342–53.

PRICE, H.H. *Belief* (The Gifford Lectures delivered at the University of Aberdeen in 1960), series 1, lecture 7. London.
[*M* 79 (1970) 454–60; *PPR* 35 (1975) 376–84]

PRUFER, T. 'Ancients and Moderns: Notes on Interpreting Hume', *Studies in Phil. & Hist. Phil.* 4, 67–74.

PUCELLE, J. *Hume, ou L'ambiguité: Présentation, choix de textes, bibliographie.* Paris. [*Biblio. of Phil.* 17 (1970) 208]

RAPHAEL, D.D. *British Moralists, 1650–1800* (selected and edited with comparative notes and analytical index), vol. 2, 1–111. Oxford.

RAPHAEL, D.D. 'Adam Smith and "The Infection of David Hume's Society": New Light on an old controversy, together with the text of a hitherto unpublished manuscript', *J. Hist. Ideas* 30, 225–48.

ROLLIN, B.E. 'Thomas Brown's Criticism of Hume on Causation', *Arch. Gesch. Phil.* 51, 85–103.

RONCHETTI, E. 'Gli studi humiani in Italia dal '35 a oggi', *Cultura e scuola* 29, 109–16.

ROSS, I. '*Le Bon David* again: Three new Hume letters', *Texas Studies in Lit. & Lang.* 10, 537–45.

ROSS, I. 'Hume and Kames—A Rejoinder', *Studies in Scott. Lit.* (U. of S. Carolina) 6, 186–9. (on McGuinness above)

ROSS, J.F. *Philosophical Theology*, 92–100. Indianapolis & New York.

SANTUCCI, A. *Sistema e ricerca in David Hume.* (296 pp.) Turin.
[*G. crit. Fil. ital.* 48 (1969) 587–96; *Studi int. Fil.* 4 (1972) 223–5]

SCHLERETH, T.J. *The cosmopolitan ideal in enlightenment thought: its form and function in the ideas of Franklin, Hume and Voltaire, 1694–1790.* U. of Iowa (diss.).

SOLON, T.P.M. & WERTZ, S.K. 'Hume's Argument from Evil', *The Personalist* 50, 383–92.

SPIEGEL, C.R. *The metaethics of David Hume.* U. of Cincinnati (diss.).

SWINBURNE, R.G. 'Whole and Part in Cosmological Arguments', *Philosophy* 44, 339–40.

VERGEZ, A. *Hume* (93 pp.) Paris. (partly excerpts, in French transl.)
[*Biblio. of Phil.* 16 (1969) 205; *Riv. Fil.* 61 (1970) 328–30]

VICKERS, J. 'Judgment and Belief', in K. Lambert, *The Logical Way of Doing Things*, 39–64. New Haven & London.

WALL, G. B. 'The specter of Hume', *Zygon* 4, 268–73.

WILLIAMS, C. J. F. 'Are Primary Qualities Qualities ?', *Phil. Q.* 19, 310–23.

WILLIAMS, M. E. 'The Breach, Again', *Ratio* 11, 79–81. (on Beck 1967) [82–7]

WOLFF, R. P. *The Essential David Hume*. New York. (anthol.)

[**1970**]

ARMSTRONG, R. L. *Metaphysics and British Empiricism*, ch. 7. Lincoln, Neb.

AUNE, B. 'The Paradox of Empiricism', *Metaphilosophy* 1, 128–38.

BANERJEE, C. *Locke and Hume in the philosophical comedy of Tristram Shandy*. Kent State U. (diss.).

BEAUCHAMP, T. L. *Hume's theory of causation*. Johns Hopkins U. (diss.).

BEVAN, J. & PRICE, J. V. 'Another copy of Hume's *Abstract*', *Book Collector* 19, 382.

BRAUDY, L. B. *Narrative Form in History and Fiction: Hume, Fielding & Gibbon*. Princeton.
[*Enlightenment Essays* 1 (1970) 70–1; *Engl. Lang. Notes* 8 (1971) 331–4; *Am. hist. Rev.* 77 (1972) 730–1]

BURKE, J. 'David Hume's Influence on Kant and its Limits', in A. Goetze & G. Pflaum, *Vergleichen und Verändern*, 350–6. Munich.

CAPALDI, N. 'Hume's Philosophy of Religion: God without Ethics', *Int. J. Phil. Relig.* 1, 233–40. (repr. 1975 as ch. 9 of his *David Hume*) [*JHP* 14 (1976) 301–11]

CARABELLI, G. 'Enlightenment Philosophy and Eighteenth Century Booktrade' [on the *Dialogues*], *Enlightenment Essays* 1, 169–78.

DONALDSON, G. L. *Hume's theory of relations*. Syracuse U. (diss.).

FALLA CÁCERES, H. *Experiencia y conocimiento en Hume*. U. Complutense, Madrid (diss.).

FORBES, D. *David Hume, The History of Great Britain* (vol. 1). Harmondsworth. (repr. of the 1st edn 1754)

FRAZER, C. S. 'Hume's Criticism and Defense of Analogical Argument', *J. Hist. Phil.* 8, 173–9.

FRAZER, C. S. 'Pattern and Predictability in Hume's *History*', *Enlightenment Essays* 1, 27–32.

GAY, P. *The Enlightenment: An Interpretation*, vol. 2, passim. London. (for vol. 1, see Gay 1966)

GRICE, G.R.; EDGLEY, R. 'Hume's Law', *Proc. Arist. Soc.* suppl. vol. 44, 89–119.

GUSTASON, W. 'Meaning and Analysis in Hume', *Man & World* 3, 49–63.

GYSENS-GOSSELIN, M. 'David Hume en Friedrich Nietzsche', *Algemeen Nederlands tijdschrift voor wijsbegeerte* 62, 108–24.

HAFTER, R.S. *Sterne's affective art and 18th century psychology*. Brandeis U. (diss.).

HALL, R. 'Yes, Hume Did Use Berkeley', *Philosophy* 45, 152–3. (reply to Conroy 1969)

HEARN, T.K. '"General Rules" in Hume's *Treatise*', *J. Hist. Phil.* 8, 405–22.

HENZE, D.F. 'On Some Alleged Humean Insights and Oversights', *Relig. Studies* 6, 369–77. (a discussion of *Dialogues* pts. X–XI, and of Pike 1963)

HILSON, J.C. 'More Unpublished Letters of David Hume', *Forum for Mod. Lang. Studies* 6, 315–26.

HUDSON, W.D. *Modern Moral Philosophy*, 249–64. London. [*J. crit. Anal.* 4 (1973) 153–8]

JONES, P. 'Another Look at Hume's Views of Aesthetic and Moral Judgments', *Phil. Q.* 20, 53–9. [21 (1971) 64–8]

KALLICH, M. *The Association of Ideas and Critical Theory in Eighteenth-Century England*, 74–95. The Hague.

KEMP, J. *Ethical Naturalism: Hobbes and Hume*, ch. 3. London.

KONRAD, A.R. 'There Is No "Fact-Value Gap" for Hume', *J. Value Inq.* 4, 126–33. [7 (1973) 52–9; 60]

LAUDAN, L.L. 'Thomas Reid and the Newtonian Turn of British Methodological Thought', in R.E. Butts & J.W. Davis, *The Methodological Heritage of Newton*, 103–31. Oxford.

LAZEROWITZ, M. 'The Problem of Justifying Induction', in Hanly & Lazerowitz, *Psychoanalysis and Philosophy*, 210–57. New York.

LYON, R. 'Notes on Hume's Philosophy of Political Economy', *J. Hist. Ideas* 31, 457–61.

MCFARLAND, J.D. *Kant's Concept of Teleology*, ch. 3 ('The Speculative Background and Hume's *Dialogues*'). Edinburgh.

MCGUINNESS, A.E. *Henry Home, Lord Kames*, ch. 3. New York.

MCRAE, R. 'Hume on Meaning', *Dialogue* 8, 486–91.

MORRISROE, M. 'Characterization as Rhetorical Device in Hume's *Dialogues* . . .', *Enlightenment Essays* 1, 95–107.

NATANSON, H. B. 'Locke and Hume: Bearings on the Legal Obligation of the Negro'. *J. Value Inq.* 5, 35–43.

NEAGOE, F. *Istoria filozofiei moderne: De la Spinoza la Diderot*, 84–102. Bucharest.

NELSON, L. *Progress and Regress in Philosophy*, vol. 1, pt. 2, esp. sec. 1 ('Hume's Psychological Critique of Metaphysical Knowledge'). Oxford. (transl. of first half of Nelson 1962)

NIELSEN, K. 'Hume and the Emotive Theory', *Phil. Studies* (Irel.) 19, 202–13. (on Sweigart 1964). Also in Spanish as 'Hume y la teoría emotiva', *Fol. Human*, 415–30.

NOXON, J. 'Senses of Identity in Hume's *Treatise*', *Dialogue* 8, 367–84.

PEARL, L. 'Hume's Criticism of the Design Argument', *The Monist* 54, 270–84.

PIKE, N. *David Hume, Dialogues concerning natural religion.* Indianapolis and New York. (contains Pike, 'Hume on the argument from design', on pp. 127–238)
[*RS* 9 (1973) 237–8]

POPKIN, R. H. 'Hume and Isaac de Pinto', *Texas Studies in Lit. & Lang.* 12, 417–30.

RISSE, W. *Die Logik der Neuzeit*, vol. 2 (1640–1780), 493–8. Stuttgart.

ROMA, E., III. '"Ought"—"Is" and the Demand for Explanatory Completeness', *J. Value Inq.* 4, 302–7.

RUBLE, R. S. *Kant's second analogy and Hume's theory of causality.* U. of Wisconsin (diss.).

SAPADIN, E. *Hume's arguments against ethical rationalism.* Claremont Grad. Sch. (diss.).

STOVE, D. 'Deductivism', *Australas. J. Phil.* 48, 76–98.
[49 (1971) 146–51]

STRAWSON, P. F. 'Imagination and Perception', in Lawrence Foster & J. W. Swanson, *Experience & Theory*, 31–54. Cambridge, Mass. (repr. 1974 in Strawson, *Freedom and Resentment*, London)

SWINBURNE, R. G. *The Concept of Miracle*, esp. ch. 2. London.

TAGLIABUE, G. M. 'Le nozione del gusto nel XVIII secolo: Davide Hume', *Rivista di Estetica* 15, 161–207.

TRANDAFOIU, N. *Critica conceptelor de substanță și cauzalitate la empiriștii englezi. Locke, Berkeley și Hume.* Babeș-Bolyai U., Cluj (diss.)

VANDER VEER, G. L. *Bradley's Metaphysics and the Self*, ch. 11. New Haven & London.

VARGISH, T. *Newman: The Contemplation of Mind*, 16–23. Oxford.

VERCRUYSSE, J. 'Lettre et corrections inédites de David Hume',
Dix-huitième siècle 2, 33–7.
WALLACE, R. C. 'Hume, Flew, and the Miraculous', *Phil. Q.* 20,
230–43. (on Flew 1961 — *Hume's Philosophy of Belief*)
WERTZ, S. K. *Humean models of historical discourse.*
U. of Oklahoma (diss.).

[**1971**]

AARON, R. I. *Knowing and the Function of Reason*, 220–37
(on causality). Oxford.
ADDANTE, P. *David Hume e il saggio dei miracoli.* (47 pp.) Bari.
[*Revue d'Hist. et de Phil. Religieuse* 52 (1972) 239–40;
Revue Mét. 80 (1975) 287]
ALLEN, H. J. 'Berkeley's Notions and Hume's Problems',
Phil. Forum 2, 371–83.
ANSCOMBE, G. E. M. *Causality and Determination.* Cambridge.
(repr. 1975 in Sosa, *Causation and Conditionals*)
ARONSON, J. 'The legacy of Hume's analysis of causation',
Studies in Hist. & Phil. of Sci. 2, 135–56.
ATTFIELD, R. 'Talents, Abilities, and Virtues', *Philosophy* 46,
255–7.
BACZKO, B. 'Hume: natura ludzka i nieobecność absolutu',
Archiwum Historii Filozofii i Myśli Społecznej 17, 207–69.
BARIDON, M. 'Une lettre inédite d'Edward Gibbon à
Jean-Baptiste-Antoine Suard', *Études anglaises* 24, 79–87.
BENNETT, J. F. *Locke, Berkeley, Hume: Central Themes.*
Oxford.
[*D* 11 (1972) 115–22; *P* 47 (1972) 175–6;
PQ 23 (1973) 73–6; *PR* 83 (1974) 126–31;
AGP 56 (1974) 113]
BEROFSKY, B. *Determinism*, ch. 7. Princeton.
BETTY, L. S. 'The Buddhist-Humean parallels: Postmortem',
Phil. East & West 21, 237–53.
BJELKE, J. F. *Intuisjon og natur*, ch. 7, 135–83. Oslo.
BREAZEALE, J. D. *Towards a nihilist epistemology: Hume and
Nietzsche.* Yale U. (diss.).
BURNS, R. M. *David Hume and miracles in historical perspective.*
Princeton U. (diss.).
CAPPIELLO, I. *La morale della simpatia in David Hume.*
(128 pp.) Naples.
CASTIGNONE, S. 'Naturalismo o emotivismo? Un dilemma
dell' etica humeana', *Riv. Fil.* 62, 69–89. [63 (1973) 257–65]
COHEN, L. J. *The Implications of Induction*, 188–92. London.

COLVER, A.W. 'Hume's *Essays*', let. to *TLS* (1 Jan.) 15.
(cf. Chapman 1928 and Colver 1974)

DELEULE, D. *David Hume, Abrégé du traité de la nature humaine.*
Texte original avec présentation, traduction et notes. Paris.
[*Étud. phil.* 27 (1972) 266–9]

DUERLINGER, J. 'The Verbal Dispute in Hume's *Dialogues*',
Arch. Gesch. Phil. 53, 22–34. [56 (1974) 239–56]

EBBING, H. 'Hume og den fenomenologiske metode. Et bidrag
til universaliestriden' (Hume and the phenomenological
method. A contribution to the controversy over universals).
Norsk Filosofisk Tidsskrift 6, 69–100.

EBERWEIN, R. 'James Beattie and David Hume on the
Imagination and Truth', *Texas Studies in Lit. & Lang.* 12,
595–603.

ENES, J. 'Ocultamento do Ser do Eu em David Hume',
Didaskalia 1, 217–31.

FLEW, A. *An Introduction to Western Philosophy*, esp. chs. 3
('The Nature of Value') and 11 ('Rationalism and
Empiricism'). London.

GIARRIZZO, G. 'Ancora su Hume storico', *Riv. stor. ital.* 83,
439–49.

GOTTERBARN, D. 'Hume's Two Lights on Cause', *Phil. Q.* 21,
168–71.

GOTTERBARN, D. *Hume's theory of relations.* Rochester U.
(diss.).

HALBERSTADT, W.H. 'A Problem in Hume's Aesthetics',
J. Aesth. & Art Crit. 30, 209–14.

HALL, R. *A Hume Bibliography, from* 1930. (80 pp.) York.
[*Philol. Q.* 51 (1972) 698; *RM* 26 (1973) 535;
Revue phil. (1974) 468]

HANNAY, A. *Mental Images, A Defence*, 127–39. London.

HARPLEY, F.N. 'Hume's Probabilism', *Australas. J. Phil.* 49,
146–51. (on Stove 1970)

HASSLER, D.M. 'David Hume and Erasmus Darwin's
Zoonomia', *Studies in Scott. Lit.* 8, 190–3.

HOPPE, H. 'Kants Antwort auf Hume', *Kant-Studien* 62,
335–50.

JAEGER, W. *Politische Partei und parlamentarische Opposition:
Eine Studie zum politischen Denken von Lord Bolingbroke und
David Hume.* Berlin.

JOJA, A. *Studii de logică*, vol. 3, 213–21 ('Skepsis. Hume şi
Kant'). Bucharest.

KAMPF, L. 'Gibbon and Hume', in S.P. Rosenbaum, *English Literature and British Philosophy*, 109–18. Chicago & London. (repr. from pp. 80–90 of his *On Modernism*, 1967)

LECALDANO, E. *Introduzione alle opere filosofiche di D. Hume.* (95 pp.) Bari.

LIVINGSTON, D.W. 'Hume on Ultimate Causation', *Am. phil. Q.* 8, 63–70.

MADDEN, E.H. 'Hume and the Fiery Furnace', *Phil. Sci.* 38, 64–78.

MADDEN, E.H. & HARE, P.H. 'The Powers That Be', *Dialogue* 10, 12–31.

MALL, R.A. 'Humes Prinzipien- und Kants Kategoriensystem', *Kant-Studien* 62, 319–34. (transl. 1975 as ch. 3 of his *Naturalism and Criticism*)

MAY, W.E. 'Knowledge of Causality in Hume and Aquinas', *The Thomist* 34, 254–88.

MIJUSKOVIC, B. 'Hume and Shaftesbury on the Self', *Phil. Q.* 21, 324–36. [23 (1973) 67–72]

MILLER, E.F. 'Hume's contribution to behavioral science', *J. Hist. behav. Sci.* 7, 154–68.

MITCHELL, D.W. 'Analysis in Theravāda Buddhism', *Phil. East & West* 21, 23–31.

MORITZ, P.A. 'Is Hume the End ?', *Phil. J.* 8, 122–30.

MUNSAT, S. 'Hume's Argument That Causes Must Precede Their Effects', *Phil. Studies* 22, 24–6.

O'HIGGINS, J. 'Hume and the Deists: a contrast in religious approaches', *J. theol. Studies* 22, 479–501.

POPPER, K.R. 'Conjectural Knowledge: My Solution of the Problem of Induction', *Revue int. Phil.* 25, 167–97. (repr. 1972 in Popper, *Objective Knowledge*)

ROLLIN, B.E. 'Hume's Blue Patch and the Mind's Creativity', *J. Hist. Ideas* 32, 119–28.

RONCHETTI, E. 'Hume meccanicista e materialista ?', *Riv. crit. Stor. Fil.* 26, 21–51.

RYLE, G. 'Hume', in Ryle, *Collected Papers*, vol. 1, 158–66. London. (reprint, in Eng. transl., of Ryle 1956)

SANTUCCI, A. *Introduzione a Hume.* Bari.

STACK, M.F. *Hume and the external world.* Duke U. (diss.).

STEGMÜLLER, W. 'Das Problem der Induktion: Humes Herausforderung und moderne Antworten', in H. Lenk, *Neue Aspekte der Wissenschaftstheorie.* Brunswick.

STERN, G. *A Faculty Theory of Knowledge: The aim and scope of Hume's first 'Enquiry'.* (155 pp.) Lewisburg.

STOCKTON, C. N. 'David Hume among the Historiographers', *Studies in Hist. & Soc.* 3, 14–24.

STOCKTON, C. N. 'Hume—Historian of the English Constitution', *Eighteenth-Century Studies* 4, 277–93,

STOCKTON, C. N. 'Are There Natural Rights in *The Federalist* ?', *Ethics* 82, 72–82.

TANAKA, T. 'Hume to James Steuart no *Principles of Political Economy*' (Hume and Steuart's *Principles*), *Keizaigaku Ronkyū* 25, no. 1.

TANAKA, T. *Shakai Kagakusha to shite no Hume* (David Hume as a Social Scientist). Tokyo.

TAYLOR, G. 'Hume's Views of Moral Judgments', *Phil. Q.* 21, 64–8.

WALLACE, K. 'A Re-Examination of Hume's Essay On Miracles', *New Scholasticism* 45, 487–90.

WEXLER, V. G. *David Hume: historian*. Columbia U. (diss.).

WOOD, F. E. 'Hume's Philosophy of Religion as reflected in the *Dialogues*', *S.-west. J. Phil.* 2, 186–93.

[1972]

ALLENTUCK, M. E. 'David Hume and Allan Ramsay: A New Letter', *Studies in Scott. Lit.* 9, 265–6.

ALLISON, H. E. 'Transcendental Affinity—Kant's Answer to Hume', in L. W. Beck, *Proc. Third int. Kant Congress*, 203–11. Dordrecht.

ÁRDAL, P. S. *David Hume, A Treatise of Human Nature, Books II and III*. London. (cf. Macnabb 1962) [Selby-Bigge text: see Nidditch 1976]

AYER, A. J. *Probability and Evidence*, 3–26. London.

BARNES, J. *The Ontological Argument*, ch. 2. London.

BARONCELLI, F. 'Di una possibile lettura demistificante dei *Dialoghi . . . di Hume*', *Proteus* 3, 35–49.

BENNETT, J. O. '*Necessary Connection*': a critique of Hume's analysis and its contemporary adherents. Tulane U. (diss.).

BRETT, N. 'Substance and Mental Identity in Hume's *Treatise*', *Phil. Q.* 22, 110–25.

BUXBAUM, M. H. 'Hume, Franklin and America: A matter of loyalties', *Enlightenment Essays* 3, 93–105.

CAPALDI, N. 'The Copernican Revolution in Hume and Kant', in L. W. Beck, *Proc. Third int. Kant Congr.* 234–40. Dordrecht.

CARABELLI, G. *Hume, e la retorica dell' ideologia: uno studio dei 'Dialoghi sulla religione naturale'*. Florence. [*Boll. fil.* 7 (1973) 134–5]

CHAPPELL, V. C. 'Hume on What There Is', in *Reason & Reality* (R. Inst. of Phil. Lectures, vol. 5), 88–98. London.

CHAVES, E. O. C. *David Hume's philosophical critique of theology and its significance for the history of Christian thought.* U. of Pittsburgh (diss.).

DELEUZE, G. 'Hume', in F. Châtelet, *Histoire de la philosophie*, vol. 4. Paris.

DODSON, D. P. *Whitehead's misapprehension of Hume.* Grad. Theol. Union (diss.).

EID, L. V. 'Taming the Agnostic: Hume and the Scottish Enlightenment', *U. of Dayton Rev.* 19, 13–24.

EMBREE, L. E. *The 'true philosophy' in Hume's 'Treatise'.* New School for Soc. Res. (diss.).

FRAZER, C. S. 'Hume on Imagination and Natural Relations', *Studies in Burke & His Time* 13, 211–18.

GINSBERG, R. 'David Hume versus the Enlightenment', *Studies on Voltaire & the 18th Century* 88, 599–650.

GOLDSTICK, D. 'Hume's "Circularity" Charge against Inductive Reasoning', *Dialogue* 11, 258–66.

GONZÁLEZ-BERENGUER, J. L. 'Un administrador preocupado por los problemas económicos: David Hume', in *Estudios en homenaje al profesor López Rodó*, vol. 3, 43–55. Madrid.

GOVIER, T. 'Variations on *Force* and *Vivacity* in Hume', *Phil. Q.* 22, 44–52.

HUFF, T. 'Self-Interest and Benevolence in Hume's Account of Moral Obligation', *Ethics* 83, 58–70.

HUNTLEY, W. B. 'David Hume and Charles Darwin', *J. Hist Ideas* 33, 457–70.

JONES, P. 'Hume's Two Concepts of God', *Philosophy* 47, 322–33.

KUHNS, R. 'Hume's Republic and the Universe of Newton', in P. Gay, *Eighteenth Century Studies Presented to Arthur M. Wilson*, 73–95. Hanover (USA).

LANGTRY, B. 'Hume on Testimony to the Miraculous', *Sophia* 11, 20–5.

LITTLE, I. L. 'Reflections on Hume's and the Buddha's ideas about the soul', *Proc. New Mexico-West Texas Phil. Soc.*, 79–84.

McELROY, E. W. *The nature of experience and the role of god: Whitehead's response to Hume.* U. of Georgia (diss.)

McMAHON, D. B. S. *David Hume's philosophy of religion.* U. of Wisconsin (diss.).

McPHERSON, T. *The Argument from Design*, passim. London.

MERCER, P. *Sympathy and Ethics: A study of the relationship between sympathy and morality, with special reference to Hume's 'Treatise'.* Oxford.

[*PQ* 22 (1972) 363–4; *D* 12 (1973) 124–7; *P* 48 (1973) 399–401; *PR* 82 (1973) 537–9]

MORRISROE, M., JR. 'Hume's Ecclesiastical History: A New Letter', *Engl. Studies* 53, 431–3.

NATHAN, G. J. *Hume's 'genuine theism and religion'.* U. of Toronto (diss.).

NEGULESCU, P. P. *Scrieri inedite*, vol. 3, 259–77. Bucharest.

NELSON, J. O. 'Two Main Questions Concerning Hume's *Treatise* and *Enquiry*', *Phil. Rev.* 81, 335–50.
[82 (1973) 371–9]

PASSMORE, J. 'Hume, David', in C. C. Gillispie, *Dictionary of Scientific Biography* (vol. 6, 555–60). New York.

POPPER, K. R. *Objective Knowledge*, 85–101 ('An Afterthought on Induction'). Oxford.

REICHENBACH, B. R. *The Cosmological Argument*, ch. 2 ('Causation'). Springfield, Ill.

ROSS, I. S. *Lord Kames and the Scotland of his Day*, esp. 75–87. Oxford.

SHANAB, R. E. A. 'Ghazali, Berkeley and Hume on causation', *Agora* 2, 16–23.

SMITH, N. 'Hume's "Rejected" Essays', *Forum for Mod. Lang. Studies* 8, 354–71.

STAFFORD, J. M. *Hume, Reid, and the uniformity of morals.* U. of Sheffield (diss.).

VITALE, J. *Kant and Hume on the a priori validity of the causal principle.* U. of Wisconsin (diss.).

WALSH, W. H. 'Hume's Concept of Truth', in *Reason & Reality* (R. Inst. of Phil. Lectures, vol. 5), 99–116.

WERNER, J. M. 'David Hume and America', *J. Hist. Ideas* 33, 439–56.

WERTZ, S. K. 'Hume's Use of the Game Analogy', *S.-west. J. Phil.* 3, 127–35.

WOOLHOUSE, R. S. 'From Conceivability to Possibility', *Ratio* 14, 144–54. [17 (1975) 118–21]

[**1973**]

ACTON, H. B. 'The Enlightenment et ses adversaires' in Y. Belaval, *Histoire de la philosophie*, vol. 2, esp. 651–64. Paris.

AHERN, D. M. *Hume on the evidential impossibility of miracles.* U. of Calif., Irvine (diss.).

ANSCOMBE, G.E.M. 'Hume and Julius Caesar', *Analysis* 34, 1–7. [35 (1974) 13–19]

ANSCOMBE, G.E.M. '"Whatever has a beginning of existence must have a cause": Hume's argument exposed', *Analysis* 34, 145–51. [35 (1974) 57–62]

ARCHER, R.H. *Hume and Sartre on the self.* Rice U. (diss.).

ARMSTRONG, D.M. *Belief, Truth and Knowledge*, 70–6 ('Hume's Problem': the distinction between a belief and a 'mere thought'). Cambridge.

AYER, A.J. *The Central Questions of Philosophy*, passim. London.

BAUM, R.J. *Philosophy and Mathematics*, ch. 9. San Francisco. (mainly excerpts)

BEAUCHAMP, T.L. 'Hume's Two Theories of Causation', *Arch. Gesch. Phil.* 55, 281–300.

BEAUCHAMP, T.L. 'No "Fact-Value Gap" for Hume?: A Reply to Konrad', *J. Value Inquiry* 7, 52–9. (on Konrad 1970)

BOTWINICK, A.I. *Ethics, politics and epistemology, a study in the unity of Hume's thought.* Princeton U. (diss.).

BRANDT, R. *David Hume, Ein Traktat über die menschliche Natur.* Deutsch ... von T. Lipps (1904 & 1906); unveränderter Nachdruck ... mit neuer Einführung ... Hamburg.

BRICKE, J. 'Hume's Theories of Dispositional Properties', *Am. phil. Q.* 10, 15–24.

BROCKWAY, G.M. *Leibniz, Hume, Kant and the contemporaries on the problem of evil*, ch. 2. U. of Wisconsin (diss.).

BROWN, S.C. *Political Obligation*, sec. 2 ('Two theories of political obligation'). Bletchley.

CLACK, R.J. 'Chisholm and Hume on Observing the Self', *Phil. & phenomenol. Res.* 33, 338–49. (on Chisholm 1969) [35 (1975) 257–60]

COADY, C.A.J. 'Testimony and Observation', *Am. phil. Q.* 10, 149–56.

COLVER, W. 'A Variant of Hume's Advertisement Repudiating the *Treatise*', *Papers of the Biblio. Soc. of Am.* 67, 66–8.

CORCORAN, C.M. 'Do we Have a Shaftesburean Self in the *Treatise*?', *Phil. Q.* 23, 67–72. (on Mijuskovic 1971)

CUMMINS, P.D. 'Hume's Disavowal of the *Treatise*', *Phil. Rev.* 82, 371–9. (on Nelson 1972)

CUMMINS, P.D. 'Locke's Anticipation of Hume's use of "impression"', *Mod. Schoolman* 50, 297–301.

DAL PRA, M. *Hume e la scienza della natura umana.* (424 pp.)
Rome & Bari. (2nd edn of Dal Pra 1949)
[*Riv. Fil. neo-scolastica* 67 (1975) 603–6]

DANTO, A.C. *Analytical Philosophy of Action*, ch. 4
('Causality and Basic Actions'). Cambridge.

DAVIE, G.E. *The Social Significance of the Scottish Philosophy of
Common Sense.* (Dow Lecture) Dundee.

DORMAN, L.M. *David Hume and the miracles controversy,
1749–1800.* U. of Calif., San Diego (diss.).

DRISCOLL, J. 'Unity, Succession, and Personal Identity in
Hume', *Studies in Phil. & Hist. Phil.* 6, 121–34.

GLOSSOP, R.J. 'On Understanding the Ethics of David Hume',
Riv. Fil. 63, 257–65. (on Castignone 1971)

GOTTERBARN, D. 'Hume's Troublesome Relations',
S.-west. J. Phil. 4, 119–24.

GOTTERBARN, D. 'How Can Hume Know Philosophical
Relations ?', *J. crit. Anal.* 4, 133–41.

GRAVEL, P. 'Hume et le miracle', *Étud. phil.* 46, 19–41.

GRAY, B.J. *An interpretation of the moral philosophy of David
Hume: how to derive 'ought' from 'is'.* Syracuse U. (diss.).

HANFLING, O. *Cause and Effect*, passim. Bletchley.

HEARN, T.K., JR. 'Árdal on the Moral Sentiments in Hume's
Treatise', *Philosophy* 48, 288–92. (on Árdal 1966)

HEARN, T.K., JR. 'MacIntyre and Hudson on Hume',
J. crit. Anal. 4, 153–8. (on MacIntyre 1959, and Hudson 1970)

HENZE, D.F. 'Hume, *Treatise* III, i, 1', *Philosophy* 48, 277–83.
(on MacIntyre 1959)

HIORTH, F. *David Hume: Liv og filosofi.* Oslo, Bergen & Tromsø.

JESSOP, T.E. 'Sur l'interprétation de Hume', *Étud. phil.* 46,
3–18.

JOHANSON, A.A. 'A proof of Hume's separation thesis based on
a formal system for descriptive and normative statements',
Theory and Decision 3, 339–49.

JOHNSON, A.L. *Religion in the age of reason: a philosophical
study of the religious views of David Hume.* U. of Nebraska
(diss.).

LESHER, J.H. 'Hume's Analysis of "Cause" and the
"Two-Definitions" Dispute', *J. Hist. Ideas* 33, 387–92.
[*JHP* 14 (1976) 99–100]

LETWIN, S. 'La philosophie de Hume', *Revue phil.* 48, 257–83.

LIVINGSTON, D.W. 'Hume on the Problem of Historical and
Scientific Explanation', *New Scholasticism* 47, 38–67.

MALL, R.A. *Experience and Reason: The Phenomenology of
Husserl and its Relation to Hume's Philosophy.* The Hague.

MICHAUD, A. 'Remarques sur le phénoménalisme et l'atomisme de D. Hume', *Étud. phil.* 46, 43–57.

MORRISROE, M., JR. 'Did Hume read Berkeley ? A conclusive answer', *Philol. Q.* 52, 310–15.

NORDGULEN, G. 'New Spokesmen in an Old Dialogue', *New Scholasticism* 47, 324–38.

NOXON, J. *Hume's Philosophical Development: A study of his methods.* (xiv, 197 pp.) Oxford.
[*RPL* 71 (1973) 367; *ASM* 8 (1973) 82–5; *PB* 15 (1974) no. 1, 16–18; *Riv. Fil.* 64 (1974) 370–2; *Phil.J.* 11 (1974) 36–9;*JHP* 13 (1975) 259–60; *P* 50 (1975) 213–14]

PATON, M. 'Hume on tragedy', *Br.J. Aesth.* 13, 121–32.

PRICE, J.V. 'Hume's "Account of Stewart": an important presentation copy', *The Bibliotheck* 6, 199–202.

RÁBADE ROMEO, S. 'Fenomenismo y yo personal en Hume', *Anales del Seminario de Metafísica* 8, 7–36.

RÁBADE ROMEO, S. 'La noción de experiencia en el empirismo inglés: Hume', *Diálogos* 9, 33–51.

RAPHAEL, D.D. 'Hume and Adam Smith on justice and utility', *Proc. Arist. Soc.* 73, 87–103.

ROBERTS, T.A. *The Concept of Benevolence*, ch. 3. London.

ROBISON, W.L. 'Hume's Scepticism', *Dialogue* 12, 87–99.

ROBISON, W.L. 'On the Consequential Claim that Hume is a Pragmatist', *J. crit. Anal.* 4, 141–53. (on Bayley 1936)

SALAS ORTUETA, J. DE 'Teoría del conocimiento y acción en la "Enquiry concerning the Human Understanding" de Hume', *Anales del Seminario de Metafísica* 8, 37–51.

SHARKEY, P.W. *Hume's theory of space and time.* U. of Notre Dame (diss.).

STOVE, D.C. *Probability and Hume's Inductive Scepticism.* Oxford.
[*D* 12 (1973) 735–41; *PQ* 24 (1974) 72–3; *PB* 15 (1974) no. 2, 24–6; *Philosophia* 4 (1974) 375–9; *AJP* 52 (1974) 269–76;*JHP* 13 (1975) 413–15; *Br.J. Phil. Sci.* 26 (1975) 85–7; *Hume Studies* 1 (1975) 25–9; *PR* 84 (1975) 453–7; *Analysis* 36 (1975) 43–6; *M* 85 (1976) 297–8; *Can.J. Phil.* 7 (1977) 203–11; *AJP* 55 (1977) 69–73; 74–5; *Ratio* 19 (1977) 47–54]

STOVE, D.C. 'An error in Selby-Bigge's *Hume*', *Australas.J. Phil.* 51, 77.

VÁMOSI, P. *Hume: Tanulmány az emberi ertelemröl* (transl. of the first *Enquiry*), with postscript and notes by M. Szenczi. Budapest.

VAN STEENBURGH, E.W. 'Hume's Ontology', *J. crit. Anal.* 4, 164–72.

VESEY, G.N.A. *Personal Identity*, 9–22 ('Hume and the unity question'). Bletchley.

WALTON, D. 'The Contemporary Relevance of Hume's Remarks on Liberty and Necessity', *J. Thought* 8, 183–8.

WALTON, D. 'Hume Exhumed: A Polemic Against Determinism', *J. crit. Anal.* 4, 159–64.

[**1974**]

ANDIC, M. '"Experimental theism" and the verbal dispute in Hume's *Dialogues*', *Arch. Gesch. Phil.* 56, 239–56.

ANSCOMBE, G.E.M. 'Times, Beginnings and Causes', *Proc. Br. Acad.* 60, 253–70.

AQUILA, R.E. 'Brentano, Descartes and Hume on Awareness', *Phil. & phenomenol. Res.* 35, 223–39.

ASHLEY, J. & STACK, M. 'Hume's Theory of the Self and its Identity', *Dialogue* 13, 239–54.
[*RM* 30 (1976) 19–38; *D* 15 (1976) 664–72]

AUGROS, R. *Hume and the problem of the existence of substance.* U. Laval (diss.).

BALDINOTTI, C. 'Dissertazione in cui spiegasi il piacere che si prova alle rappresentazioni tragiche', *Riv. crit. Stor. Fil.* 29 171–90. (edited by M. Dal Pra.)

BATTESTIN, M.C. 'The Problem of *Amelia*: Hume, Barrow, and the Conversion of Captain Booth', *Engl. lit. Hist.* 41, 613–48.

BEAUCHAMP, T.L. 'Hume on Causal Contiguity and Causal Succession', *Dialogue* 13, 271–82.

BECK, L.W. '"Was-must be" and "is-ought" in Hume', *Phil. Studies* 26, 219–28.

BENNETT, J.O. 'A Process View of Causality', *Tulane Studies in Phil.* 23, 1–12.

BOUVERESSE, R. *David Hume, Les essais esthétiques.* 2 vols. Paris. (vol. I publ. in 1973.)
[*RPL* 72 (1974) 292–3; *RIP* 29 (1975) 187–9; *RPL* 74 (1976) 126–9; *RP* 166 (1976) 316–18]

BRANDT, R. *Eigentumstheorien von Grotius bis Kant*, 104–44. Stuttgart.

BRETT, N. 'Scepticism and Vain Questions', *Dialogue* 13, 657–73.

BRICKE, J. 'Hume's Conception of Character', *S.-west. J. Phil.* 5, 107–13.

BRICKE, J. 'Emotion and Thought in Hume's *Treatise*', *Canadian J. Phil.* suppl. vol. 1, 53–71. (repr. 1975 in T. Penelhum & R. Shiner, *New Essays in the History of Philosophy*)

BRICKE, J. 'Hume's Associationist Psychology', *J. Hist. behav. Sci.* 10, 397–409.

BROOKE, J. H., et al. *New Interactions between Theology and Natural Science*, ch. 7 ('Hume and the Rationality of Natural Theology'). Milton Keynes.

BURNS, H. R. *Hume's attitude towards religion*. St Louis U. (diss.).

CLARKE, B. L. 'The Argument from Design: A piece of abductive reasoning', *Int. J. Phil. Relig.* 5, 65–78.

COLVER, A. W. 'The "First" Edition of Hume's *Essays and Treatises*', *Papers of the Biblio. Soc. of Am.* 68, 39–44.

CREGAN, M. 'David Hume, the Christian ?', *New Blackfriars* 55, 325–9.

DAL PRA, M.: see Baldinotti.

DAVID, M. 'Histoire des religions et philosophie au XVIIIe siècle: le Président de Brosses, David Hume et Diderot', *Revue phil.* 99, 145–60.

DEITSCH, M. 'The Observability of the Self', *Phil. Studies* 26, 69–71. (on Chisholm 1969)

DIXON, J. E. *Reason and sympathy in Hume's 'Treatise'*. U. of Br. Columbia (diss.).

DMOCHOWSKI, H. W. *The moral philosophy of David Hume and the 'is-ought' question*. New York U. (diss.).

FERGUSON, J. P. *The Philosophy of Dr. Samuel Clarke, and its critics*, 111–21 and 218–30. New York, etc.

FLEW, A. G. N. 'Was Berkeley a Precursor of Wittgenstein ?', in Todd, 153–63.

GASKIN, J. C. 'God, Hume, and Natural Belief', *Philosophy* 49, 281–94. (partly on Butler 1960)

GENOVA, A. C. 'On Anscombe's exposition of Hume', *Analysis* 35, 57–62. (on Anscombe 1973b)

GOTTERBARN, D. 'Kant, Hume and analyticity', *Kant-Studien* 65, 274–83.

GULIAN, C. I. *Introducere în istoria filozofiei moderne*, 171–83. Bucharest.

HALL, R. 'Hume's Use of Locke on Identity', *The Locke Newsletter* 5, 56–75.

HASKIN, D. 'English Bards and a Scottish Previewer', *New Blackfriars* 55, 33–42.

HENRY, W. L. *A study of David Hume versus his eighteenth-century English contemporaries on the question of natural theology.* Vanderbilt U. (diss.).

HUNDERT, E. J. 'The Achievement Motive in Hume's Political Economy', *J. Hist. Ideas* 35, 139–43.

HUNTER, G. B. B. 'Concepts and Meaning', in Todd, 136–52.

JACOBSON, A. M. J. *Causality: a discussion of the analysis of this notion, with some criticisms of the Humean account.* Oxford U. (diss.).

JEDYNAK, S. *Hume.* [Polish.] (231 pp.) Warsaw.

JESSOP, T. E. 'Hume, David', in the *Encyclopaedia Britannica,* 15th edn (vol. 8, 1191–4).

JESSOP, T. E. 'The Misunderstood Hume'; in Todd, 1–13.

LAND, S. K. 'Universalism and Relativism: A Philosophical Problem of Translation in the Eighteenth Century', *J. Hist. Ideas* 35, 597–610.

LAZEROWITZ, M. 'Metaphilosophy', *Critica* 5, 3–27.

LEVISON, A. B. *Knowledge and Society,* ch. 2 ('David Hume's Science of Human Nature'). Indianapolis, etc.

LIVINGSTON, D. W. 'Anscombe, Hume and Julius Caesar', *Analysis* 35, 13–19. (on Anscombe 1973a)

MACKIE, J. L. *The Cement of the Universe,* ch. 1 ('Hume's Account of Causation'). Oxford.
[*PB* 16 (1975) no. 1, 1–8; *P* 50 (1975) 362–4]

MACNABB, D. G. C. 'Michotte and Hume on Mechanical Causation', in Todd, 52–9. (on Michotte 1946)

MALL, R. A. 'Naturalismus und Kritizismus (Hume und Kant)', *Akten des 4. Internationalen Kant-Kongresses,* pt. 2, vol. 1, 30–41. Berlin & New York. (transl. 1975 as ch. 4 of his *Naturalism und Criticism.*)

MANDELBAUM, M. 'The Distinguishable and the Separable: A Note on Hume and Causation', *J. Hist. Phil.* 12, 242–7.

MARTIN, R. *Hume on personal identity.* U. of York (diss.).

MELLIZO, C. 'Hume: sobre las ideas abstractas', *Estud. de Metafísica* 4, 177–86.

MIJUSKOVIC, B. L. *The Achilles of Rationalist Arguments,* ch. 4 ('Personal Identity in the 17th and 18th Centuries'). The Hague. [*PB* 16 (1975) no. 2, 17–19]

MILLER, D. 'The Ideological Backgrounds to Conceptions of Social Justice', *Polit. Studies* 22, 387–99.

MORRISROE, M., JR. 'Linguistic Analysis as Rhetorical Pattern in David Hume', in Todd, 72–82.

MOUTON, D. L. 'Hume and Descartes on Self-Acquaintance', *Dialogue* 13, 255–69.

NOXON, J. *La evolución filosófica de Hume.* Madrid. (transl. of Noxon 1973)

NUTTALL, A.D. *A Common Sky: Philosophy and the literary imagination*, 93–111. London.

OHMORI, S. 'Beyond Hume's "Fancy"', *Revue int. Phil.* 28, 99–115.

PAPANOUTSOS, E.P. *David Hume* (Χιοῦμ) · « *Δοκίμια · Φιλολογικά, 'Ηθικά, Πολιτικά* ». (*Εἰσαγωγὴ—Μετάφραση—Σχόλια.*) [27 of the Essays] Athens.

PATTEN, S.C. *Kant's response to Hume on the unity of mind.* U. of Washington (diss.).

PETERS, R.S. 'Hume's Argument from Design', in Todd, 83–98.

POPKIN, R.H. 'Hume and Isaac de Pinto, II. Five New Letters', in Todd, 99–127.

PRICE, J.V. 'Hume and Nancy Orde. Three New Letters', in Todd, 128–35.

PRICE, J.V. 'The First Publications of David Hume's *Dialogues* . . .', *Papers of the Biblio. Soc. of America* 68, 119–27.

RAPAPORT, D. *The History of the Concept of Association of Ideas*, 122–59. New York.

RAPHAEL, D.D. 'Hume's Critique of Ethical Rationalism', in Todd, 14–29.

REDMON, R. 'Hume and Resemblance', *The Personalist* 55, 369–74.

RESTAINO, F. *Scetticismo e senso comune: La filosofia scozzese da Hume a Reid*, esp. ch. 3. Bari.

ROBISON, W.L. 'Hume on Personal Identity', *J. Hist. Phil.* 12, 182–93.

ROSS, I. 'Philosophy and Fiction. The Challenge of David Hume', in Todd, 60–71.

SHEEKS, W. 'Hume's Doctrine of Belief: Truth based on Feeling', *Midwest J. Phil.* 39–43.

SIEVERT, D. 'Hume, Secret Powers, and Induction', *Phil. Studies* 25, 247–60.

SKINNER, A.S. 'Adam Smith. Science and the Role of the Imagination', in Todd, 164–88.

STANZEL, F.K. 'Schemata und Klischees der Völkerbeschreibung in David Hume's Essay "Of National Characters"', in Buchloh, Leimberg, & Rauter, *Studien zur englischen und amerikanischen Literatur: Festschrift fur Helmut Papajewski*, 363–83. Neumünster.

STEWART, C.G. *Hume's theory of the passions.* U. of Washington (diss.).

TODD, W.B. *Hume and the Enlightenment: Essays presented to Ernest Campbell Mossner.* Edinburgh & Austin. (includes, on pp. 189–205, W.B. Todd, 'David Hume. A Preliminary Bibliography')
[*Times Higher Ed. Supp.* no. 188 (23 May 1975) 21; *TLS* (11 July 1975) 777–8; *Philol. Q.* 54 (1975) 963–5; *RCSF* 30 (1975) 214–17]

TRIVUS, S. *Space, time and measure, a study in the philosophy of David Hume.* U. of Calif., Los Angeles (diss.).

TURCO, L. *Dal Sistema al Senso comune.* Bologna.

TWEYMAN, S. *Reason and Conduct in Hume and his predecessors.* The Hague.
[*PB* 17 (1976) no. 1, 24–5; *Erasmus* 27 (1975) 781–2; *D* 15 (1976) 327–33]

TWEYMAN, S. 'Hume on Separating the Inseparable', in Todd, 30–42.

VALENT, L. *Verità e Prassi in David Hume.* Brescia.
[*Boll. fil.* 9 (1975) 34–5]

VANTERPOOL, R. 'Hume's Account of General Rules', *Sth. J. Phil.* 12, 481–92.

VESEY, G.N.A. *Personal Identity*, ch. 1 (1–12). London.
[*P* 50 (1975) 117–18; *M* 85 (1976) 143–5]

WALTON, C. 'Hume and Jefferson on the Uses of History', in C. Walton & J.P. Anton, *Philosophy and the Civilizing Arts, Essays presented to Herbert W. Schneider*, 103–25. Athens, Ohio. (repr. 1976 in Livingston & King, *Hume: A Re-evaluation*)

WIENER, P.P. 'Kant and Hume on Reason and Experience in Ethics', in Todd, 43–51.

WOLFRAM, S. 'Hume on Personal Identity', *Mind* 83, 586–93.

YEGHIAYAN, E. *Hume's theory of moral sentiments.* U. of Calif., Irvine (diss.).

[1975]

ADLER, J.E. 'Stove on Hume's Inductive Scepticism', *Australas. J. Phil.* 53, 167–70. [54 (1976) 140–7]

AGNEW, P.G. *Hume's theory of consciousness and the idealist/realist interpretation of the 'Treatise'.* Claremont Grad. Sch. (diss.).

AHERN, D.M. 'Hume on the Evidential Impossibility of Miracles', *Am. phil. Q.* Monograph no. 9, 1–31.

ANDERSON, R.F. 'Hume's Account of Knowledge of External Objects', *J. Hist. Phil.* 13, 471–80.

BAKER, K. M. *Condorcet: From Natural Philosophy to Social Mathematics*, 135–55. Chicago & London.

BARONCELLI, F. 'Primi Dubbi sul "Sistema": L'Illuminismo Anacronistico di David Hume', *Riv. Fil.* 66, 141–54.

BARONCELLI, F. *Un inquietante filosofo perbene. Saggio su David Hume*. (xii, 259 pp.) Florence.

BEAUCHAMP, T. L. & MAPPES, T. A. 'Is Hume Really a Sceptic about Induction?', *Am. phil. Q.* 12, 119–29. [*Hume Studies* 3 (1977) 1–16]

BEITZINGER, A. 'The Place of Hume in the History of Jurisprudence', *Am. J. Jurisprud.* (*Natural Law Forum*) 20, 20–37.

BELL, R. H. 'David Hume's Fables of Identity', *Philol. Q.* 54, 471–83.

BENNETT, J. O. 'Natural and Nomological Necessity', *New Scholasticism* 49, 393–409.

BOSS, G. 'Hume et Spinoza', *Revue théol. Phil.*, 227–43.

BREAZEALE, D. 'Hume's Impasse', *J. Hist. Phil.* 13, 311–33.

BRICKE, J. 'On the Interpretation of Hume's *Dialogues*', *Relig. Studies* 11, 1–18.

BURCH, R. W. 'Hume on Pride and Humility', *New Scholasticism* 49, 177–88.

BUTLER, R. J. 'T and Sympathy', *Proc. Arist. Soc.* suppl. vol. 49, 1–20.

CAPALDI, N. *David Hume: The Newtonian Philosopher*. Boston. [*Hume Studies* 2 (1976) 104–15; *PQ* 27 (1977) 172–3; *PR* 86 (1977) 391–4]

CASULLO, A. 'Conceivability and Possibility', *Ratio* 17, 118–21. (on Woolhouse 1972)

CHAMLEY, P. E. 'The Conflict between Montesquieu and Hume', in A. S. Skinner & T. Wilson, *Essays on Adam Smith*, 274–305. Oxford.

CONNON, R. W. '"A Treatise of Human Nature"', let. to *TLS* (4 Apr.) 376.

CONNON, R. W. 'Some MS Corrections by Hume in the Third Volume of his *Treatise* . . .', *Long Room* 11, 14–23.

CRAIG, E. 'Hume's Letter to Stewart', *Hume Studies* 1, 70–5. (on Stove below)

DAUER, F. W. 'Towards a Copernican Reading of Hume', *Noûs* 9, 269–93.

DUGGAN, T. 'Hume on Causation' in K. Lehrer, *Analysis and Metaphysics: Essays in Honor of R. M. Chisholm*, 173–87. Dordrecht.

ECHELBARGER, C. 'Hume's Tacit Atheism', *Relig. Studies* 11, 19–35. (partly on Nathan 1966)

FALK, W. D. 'Hume on Practical Reason', *Phil. Studies* 27, 1–18.

FORBES, D. *Hume's Philosophical Politics.* Cambridge.
[*P* 51 (1976) 368–9; *TLS* (18 June 1976) 744–5, and (23 July) 824, and (6 Aug.) 986, and (13 Aug.) 1012; *Polit. Theory* 4 (1976) 516–19; *PS* 24 (1976) 334–8; *JHP* 15 (1977) 231–3]

FORBES, D. 'Sceptical Whiggism, Commerce, and Liberty', in A. S. Skinner & T. Wilson, *Essays on Adam Smith,* 179–201. Oxford.

FORMIGARI, L. *Hume. Politica e Scienza dell' Uomo.*

GASKIN, J. C. A. 'Miracles and the Religiously Significant Coincidence', *Ratio* 17, 72–81.

GRISEZ, G. *Beyond the New Theism,* chs. 6–7 and 22. Notre Dame.

GROBMAN, N. R. 'David Hume and the Earliest Scientific Methodology for Collecting Balladry', *Western Folklore* 34, 16–31.

GUPTA, B. *The conception of the self in Hume and Buddhism.* Sth. Illinois U. (diss.).

HAAKONSSEN, K. 'Hume's Social Explanations: The Case of Justice', *Danish Yearbook of Phil.* 12, 114–28.

HACKING, I. *The Emergence of Probability,* ch. 19. Cambridge.

HARRÉ, R. & MADDEN, E. H. *Causal Powers.* Oxford.
[*Hume Studies* 2 (1976) 86–94]

HARWARD, D. W. 'Hume's *Dialogues* Revisited', *Int. J. Phil. Relig.* 6, 137–53.

HAUSMAN, A. 'Some Counsel on Humean Relations', *Hume Studies* 1, 48–65. (on Imlay below) [2 (1976) 47–52]

HILSON, J. C. 'An Early Account of David Hume', *Hume Studies* 1, 78–81.

HOWELLS, E. G. *Hume and teleology: A background study of Hume's interest in the argument from design.* Stanford U. (diss.).

HUDSON, S. 'Humean Pleasures Reconsidered', *Can. J. Phil.* 5, 545–62.

HULL, R. T. 'Some reflections occasioned by Clack and Chisholm on the Self', *Phil. & phenomenol. Res.* 35, 257–60. (on Clack 1973)

IMLAY, R. A. 'Hume on Intuitive and Demonstrative Inference', *Hume Studies* 1, 31–47. [48–65]

IRWIN, T. H. 'Aristotle on Reason, Desire, and Virtue', *J. Phil.* 72, 567–78. [579–80]

KEEN, C. N. *Naturalism, skepticism and reason in Hume's 'Treatise'*. McMaster U. (diss.).

KEKES, J. 'The Case for Scepticism', *Phil. Q.* 25, 28–39.

KILCUP, R. W. *David Hume, The History of England . . .* (abridged). (with introduction on pp. xi–liv) Chicago.

KNIGHT, T. S. 'Chisholm's Defense of the Observability of the Self', *J. crit. Anal.* 6, 13–21. (on Chisholm 1969)

KOSTJUK, V. N. [Russian title] (David Hume and the problem of 'the basis of knowledge'), *Filosofskie Nauki*, no. 2, 96–102.

LANGTRY, B. 'Hume on miracles and contrary religions', *Sophia* 14, 29–34.

LECALDANO, E. *Hume, Trattato sulla natura umana.* 2 vols. Rome & Bari.

LETWIN, S. R. 'Hume: Inventor of a New Task for Philosophy', *Polit. Theory* 3, 134–58.

MALL, R. A. 'Der Induktionsbegriff. Hume und Husserl', *Z. phil. Forschung* 29, 34–62.

MALL, R. A. *Naturalism and Criticism.* (105 pp.) The Hague.

MELCHERT, M. 'Hume's Appendix on Personal Identity', *Phil. Res. Arch.* 1, no. 1072.

MOONAN, L. 'Hume on Is and Ought', *J. Hist. Phil* 13, 83–98.

MWAIPAYA, P. A. *Belief as the foundation of Hume's philosophy.* U. of Louvain (diss.).

NAULTY, R. A. & SHEEHAN, P. J. 'Hume, Price and testimony', *Phil. & phenomenol. Res.* 35, 376–84. (on Price 1969)

NIDDITCH, P. H. *David Hume, Enquiries . . .*, ed. L. A. Selby-Bigge, 3rd edn (revised text, and notes). Oxford.
[*PB* 17 (1976) no. 1, 24–5]

NORTON, D. F. 'Hume's Common Sense Morality', *Can. J. Phil.* 5, 523–43.

OWEN, D. W. D. 'An Unnoticed Error in Hume's *Treatise*', *Hume Studies* 1, 76–7.

PANOVA, E. 'The Main Principles of David Hume's Epistemology as a Source of Contemporary Positivism', *Revolutionary World* 11, 218–27.

PEARS, D. 'Hume's Account of Personal Identity', in his *Questions in the Philosophy of Mind*, 208–23. London. (repr. 1975 in *Philosophic Exchange* 2, no. 1)

PENELHUM, T. *Hume.* (Philosophers in Perspective) London.
[*P* 51 (1976) 367–8; *Hume Studies* 2 (1976) 104–15; *PQ* 26 (1976) 268–70; *PB* 17 (1976) 62–3; *D* 15 (1976) 505–9; *ASM* 11 (1976) 178–81]

PENELHUM, T. 'Hume's Theory of the Self Revisited', *Dialogue* 14, 389–409.

PERRY, J. *Personal Identity*, introduction, 26–30.

RÁBADE ROMEO, S. *Hume y el fenomenismo moderno.* (474 pp.) Madrid. [*ASM* 11 (1976) 169–72]

RAPHAEL, D. D. *Physics and ethics: the influence of Newton on moral philosophy.* (Inaug. Lect.) London.

ROHATYN, D. A. 'Kant, Hume and Causality', *Z. allgemeine Wissenschaftstheorie* 6, 34–6.

ROSENBERG, A. 'Propter Hoc, Ergo Post Hoc', *Am. phil. Q.* 12, 235–54.

SALAS ORTUETA, J. DE. 'Metafísica y concepción de la naturaleza en Leibniz y en Hume', *Revista de la Universidad Complutense* 24, 127–50.

SHANAB, R. E. A. 'Hume on Necessity', *Indian phil. Q.* 2, 243–52.

SIEBERT, D. T., JR. 'Johnson and Hume on Miracles', *J. Hist. Ideas* 36, 543–47.

SMITH, D. S. *The unity of Hume's 'Treatise'.* Cath. U. of America (diss.).

SNARE, F. 'The Argument from Motivation', *Mind* 84, 1–9.

SPARSHOTT, F. E. 'In Defense of Kemp-Smith', *Hume Studies* 1, 66–9. (a reply to the following)

STOVE, D. C. 'Hume, The Causal Principle, and Kemp Smith', *Hume Studies* 1, 1–24. [66–9; 70–5; *AJP* 55 (1977) 59–63]

TRANDAFOIU, N. *Substanţa şi cauzalitatea în interpretarea empirismului englez*, 180–320. Cluj-Napoca.

VOIGT, U. *David Hume und das Problem der Geschichte.* Berlin & Munich.

VON SAVIGNY, E. 'Inwieweit hat Sextus Empiricus Humes Argumente gegen die Induktion vorweggenommen ?', *Arch. Gesch. Phil.* 57, 269–85.

WATERLOW, S. 'On a proposed refutation of Hume', *Analysis* 36, 43–6. (on Stove 1973a)

WATKINS, J. 'Three Views concerning Human Freedom', in R. S. Peters, *Nature and Conduct* (R. Inst. of Phil. Lectures, vol. 8), 200–28. London.

WERTZ, S. K. 'Hume, History, and Human Nature', *J. Hist. Ideas* 36, 481–96.

WRIGHT, J. P. *Mind and external existence: an analytical-historical study of a problem of Humean metaphysics.* York U., Canada (diss.).

ZANER, R. 'Hume and the Discipline of Phenomenology: An Historical Perspective', in *Phenomenological Perspectives: ... essays in honor of Herbert Spiegelberg*. (Phaenomenologica, 62) The Hague.

ZARTMAN, J. F. 'Hume and "The Meaning of a Word"', *Phil. & phenomenol. Res.* 36, 255–60.

ZEIGLER, G. M. 'Hume's View of the Causal Relation', *The Personalist* 56, 351–63. (partly on Robinson 1966)

[**1976**]

ALEJANDRO, J. M. DE. 'El atomismo gnoseológico de David Hume (1711–1776)', *Pensamiento* 32, 383–403.

ALLINSON, R. E. 'The Second Analogy Revisited: Did Kant Refute Hume ?', *J. W. Virginia phil. Soc.* 21–3.

ANDERSON, R. F. 'The Location, Extension, Shape, and Size of Hume's Perceptions', in Livingston & King (see below), 153–71.

ARCE CARRASCOSO, J. L. 'Creencia y simpatía en Hume', *Anales del Seminario de Metafísica* 11, 7–49.

ÁRDAL, P. S. 'Some Implications of the Virtue of Reasonableness in Hume's *Treatise*', in Livingston & King, 91–106.

ARDLEY, G. 'Hume's Common Sense Critics', *Revue int. Phil.* 30, 104–25.

ATKINSON, R. F. 'Hume on the Standard of Morals', in Merrill & Shahan (see below), 25–44.

BAGOLINI, L. *David Hume e Adam Smith: Elementi per una ricerca di filosofia giuridica e politica*. Bologna.

BAYLES, M. D. 'Hume on Blame and Excuse', *Hume Studies* 2, 17–35.

BEANBLOSSOM, R. E. 'A New Foundation for Humean Scepticism', *Phil. Studies* 29, 207–10.

BEAUCHAMP, T. L. 'An Analysis of Hume's Essay "On Suicide"', *Rev. Met.* 30, 73–95.

BENCE, G. *Hume: Értekezés az emberi természetröl* (transl. of the *Treatise*), with postscript and notes by M. Ludassy. Budapest.

BERMAN, D. 'David Hume on the 1641 Rebellion in Ireland', *Studies: an Ir. q. Rev.* 65, 101–12.

BIRO, J. I. 'Hume on Self-Identity and Memory', *Rev. Met.* 30, 19–38.

BJELKE, J. F. 'Wirklichkeitserkenntnis und Wirklichkeits-imagination bei Hume', *Arch. Gesch. Phil.* 58, 23–39.

BOATRIGHT, J.R. 'Hume's Account of Moral Sentiment', *Revue int. Phil.* 30, 79–90.

BOSSERT, P.J. 'Hume and Husserl on Time and Time-Consciousness', *J. Br. Soc. Phenomenol.* 7, 44–52.

BURCH, R.W. 'What is Hume's Doctrine of Negation ?' *Int. Logic Rev.* 7, 236–42.

BURNS, S. 'The Humean Female', *Dialogue* 15, 415–24. [425–40]

BUTLER, R.J. 'Distinctiones Rationis, or the Cheshire Cat which left its smile behind it', *Proc. Arist. Soc.* 76, 165–76.

BUTLER, R.J. 'Hume's Impressions', in G. Vesey, *Impressions of Empiricism* (R. Inst. of Phil. Lectures, vol.9), 122–36. London.

CAPALDI, N. 'Hume's Theory of the Passions', in Livingston & King, 172–90.

CHERRY, C. 'Nature, Artifice and Moral Approbation', *Proc. Arist. Soc.* 76, 265–82.

COHEN, R. 'The Rationale of Hume's Literary Inquiries', in Merrill & Shahan, 97–115.

COLVER, A.W. *David Hume, The Natural History of Religion* and PRICE, J.V. *David Hume, Dialogues concerning Natural Religion.* Oxford.
[*PB* 18 (1977) 49–54; *P* 52 (1977) 362–4; *TLS* (2 Aug. 1977) 984; *Hermathena* no. 123 (1977) 76–8]

CONNIFF, J. 'Hume's Political Methodology: A Reconsideration of "That Politics May Be Reduced to a Science"', *Rev. Polit.* 38, 88–108.

CONNON, R.W. 'Some Hume MS Alterations on a Copy of the *Abstract*', *J. Hist. Phil.* 14, 353–6.

COTTLE, C.E. *Some correctives on readings of Hume's theory of justice.* Kent State U. (diss.).

COURTENAY, W.J. et al. *Ockham, Descartes, and Hume: Self-Knowledge, Substance, and Causality.* Madison.

CURRÁS RÁBADE, A. 'Hume: Realidad, creencia, ficción', *Anales del Seminario de Metafísica* 11, 51–61.

DAVIDSON, D. 'Hume's Cognitive theory of Pride', *J. Phil.* 73, 744–57.

DAVIE, W. 'Hume's Catalog of Virtue and Vice', in Merrill & Shahan, 45–57.

DERATHÉ, R. 'L'obligation politique selon Hume', *Revue int. Phil.* 30, 91–103.

DÍAZ DÍAZ, G. 'David Hume en las letras españolas. Nota bibliográfica', *Anales del Seminario de Metafísica* 11, 159–63.

ESPOSITO, J.L. 'Hume and the Transcendental Idealists',
Sth.J. Phil. 14, 431–42.

FALK, W.D. 'Hume on Is and Ought', *Can.J. Phil.* 6, 359–78.

FEINSTEIN, R. 'Some New Thoughts on David Hume',
Second Order 5, 44–50.

FLEW, A. 'Three questions about justice in the *Treatise*',
Phil. Q. 26, 1–13.

FLEW, A. 'Natural Necessities and Causal Powers',
Hume Studies 2, 86–94. (on Harré & Madden 1975)
[95–103]

FLEW, A. 'Hume and Historical Necessity', *Teorema* 6, 277–309.
(repr. in revised form 1978 as ch. 3 of Flew, *A Rational
Animal*, Oxford). Also as 'Hume y la necesidad histórica' in
the Spanish version of *Teorema*, 277–310.

FOGELIN, R.J. 'Kant and Hume on Simultaneity of Causes and
Effects', *Kant-Studien* 67, 51–9.

GASKIN, J.C.A. 'The Design Argument: Hume's Critique of
Poor Reason', *Relig. Studies* 12, 331–45. (includes criticism
of Gaskin 1968)

GASKIN, J.C.A. 'Hume's Critique of Religion', *J. Hist. Phil.* 14,
301–11. (on Noxon 1964 and Capaldi 1970)

GLOSSOP, R.J. 'Hume, Stevenson, and Hare on Moral
Language', in Livingston & King, 362–85.

GLOSSOP, R.J. 'Is Hume A "Classical Utilitarian"?',
Hume Studies 2, 1–16.

GOMBERG, P. 'Coherence and Causal Inference in Hume's
Treatise', *Can.J. Phil.* 6, 693–704.

GOTTERBARN, D. 'Hume's Definition of Cause: Skepticism
with regard to Lesher's Two Senses', *J. Hist. Phil.* 14, 99–100.
(on Lesher 1973)

GRAVE, S.A. 'Hume's Criticism of the Argument from
Design', *Revue int. Phil.* 30, 64–78.

GRAY, R. 'A Refutation of Hume's Theory of Causality',
Hume Studies 2, 76–85. [3 (1977) 51–2]

GRIFFIN-COLLART, E. 'Les croyances naturelles de Hume et
les principes de sens commun de Reid', *Revue int. Phil.* 30,
126–42.

HALL, R. 'More Hume Bibliography', *Phil. Q.* 26, 92–101.
(Contains corrections and addenda to Hall, *A Hume
Bibliography, from 1930* [1971], and supplements it for the
years 1971 to 1975)

HALL, R. 'Locke and the *Abstract* of Hume', *The Locke
Newsletter* 7, 79–82.

HANFLING, O. 'Hume and Wittgenstein', in G. Vesey, *Impressions of Empiricism* (R. Inst. of Phil. Lectures, vol. 9), 47–65. London.

HARRISON, J. *Hume's Moral Epistemology*. Oxford. [*TLS* (27 Aug. 1976) 1058; *P* 52 (1977) 491–3; *PQ* 28 (1978) 77–8]

HAWKINS, R. J. 'Simplicity, resemblance and contrariety in Hume', *Phil. Q.* 26, 24–38.

HEARN, T. K. 'General Rules and the Moral Sentiments in Hume's *Treatise*', *Rev. Met.* 30, 57–72.

HEARN, T. K. 'Making Sweetbreads Do: Robert Frost and Moral Empiricism', *New England Q.* 49, 65–81.

HEATH, P. L. 'The Incredulous Hume', *Am. phil. Q.* 13, 159–63.

HERNÁNDEZ BORQUE, F. 'Hume y Merleau-Ponty, filósofos de la experiencia', *Anales del Seminario de Metafísica* 11, 63–104.

HILSON, J. C. 'A parody of Hume and its author', *Notes & Queries* 23, 352–4

HODGES, M. & LACHS, J. 'Hume on Belief', *Rev. Met.* 30, 3–18.

HOPPE, H. H. *Handeln und Erkennen. Zur Kritik des Empirismus am Beispiel der Philosophie David Humes.* Berne & Frankfurt.

IMLAY, R. A. 'Hausman on Certainty and Necessity in Hume', *Hume Studies* 2, 47–52. (on Hausman 1975)

JESSOP, T. E. 'Hume's Limited Scepticism', *Revue int. Phil.* 30, 3–27.

JOHNSON, O. A. 'Mitigated Scepticism', *Ratio* 18, 73–84.

JONES, P. 'Hume's aesthetics reassessed', *Phil. Q.* 26, 48–62.

JONES, P. 'Strains in Hume and Wittgenstein', in Livingston & King, 191–209.

JONES, P. 'Cause, Reason, and Objectivity in Hume's Aesthetics', in Livingston & King, 323–42.

KEEN, C. N. 'Reason in Hume's *Dialogues*', *Phil. Papers* 5, 121–34. (partly on Nathan 1966)

KEKES, J. *A Justification of Rationality*, ch. 1. Albany, N.Y.

KING, J. T. 'The Place of the Language of Morals in Hume's Second *Enquiry*', in Livingston & King, 343–61.

KORSMEYER, C. W. 'Hume and the Foundations of Taste', *J. Aesth. & Art Crit.* 35, 201–15.

KUNTZ, P. G. 'Hume's Metaphysics: A New Theory of Order', *Relig. Studies* 12, 401–28.

LACOSTE, L. M. 'The Consistency of Hume's Position Concerning Women', *Dialogue* 15, 425–40.

LIVINGSTON, D. W. 'Hume's Historical Theory of Meaning', in Livingston & King, 213–38.

LIVINGSTON, D. W. & KING, J. T. *Hume: A Re-evaluation.* New York. Introduction by Livingston, on pp. 1–19. (Contains reprints of Wolin 1954, Adair 1957, Flew 1967, and Walton 1974; and the new articles by Anderson, Árdal, Capaldi, Glossop, Jones, King, and Livingston listed above, and by Nathan, Noxon, Robison, Stockton, Stove, Yandell, and Zabeeh below)

LUDASSY, M. 'A természetes erények és a mesterséges igazság (Hume Értekezése az Emberi természetröl)' (The natural virtues and the artificial: justice in Hume's *Treatise*, Book III), *Magyar Filozófiai Szemle* 20, 418–46.

MACKIE, J. L. *Problems from Locke*, 145–9 ('Hume's account of identity'). Oxford.

MADDEN, E. H. & HARRÉ, R. 'Hume and Nonlogical Necessity', *Hume Studies* 2, 95–103. (reply to Flew)

MALHERBE, M. 'Le problème de l'identité dans la philosophie sceptique de David Hume', *Revue int. Phil.* 30, 28–46.

MALHERBE, M. *La Philosophie Empiriste de David Hume.* (322 pp.) Paris. [*ASM* 11 (1976) 175–8]

MERRILL, K. R. 'Hume, Whitehead, and Philosophic Method', in Merrill & Shahan, 135–60.

MERRILL, K. R. & SHAHAN, R. S. *David Hume: Many-sided Genius.* (= *S.-west. J. Phil.* 7, no. 2.) Norman, Oklahoma. (Contains the new articles by Atkinson, Cohen, Davie and Merrill listed above, and by Noxon, Penelhum, Popkin, and Rotwein below; and the translation of Reinach) [*Hume Studies* 3 (1977) 103–6]

MILLER, D. *Social Justice*, ch. 5 ('Hume's Theory of Justice'). Oxford.

MOORE, J. 'Hume's Theory of Justice and Property', *Polit. Studies* 24, 103–19.

NATHAN, G. J. 'The Existence and Nature of God in Hume's Theism', in Livingston & King, 126–49.

NATHANSON, S. 'Hume's Second Thoughts on the Self', *Hume Studies* 2, 36–46.

NELSON, J. O. 'Has the authorship of *An Abstract of A Treatise of Human Nature* really been decided?', *Phil. Q.* 26, 82–91. [*The Locke Newsletter* 7 (1976) 79–82; Nidditch (1976) 47–9; *PQ* 27 (1977) 60–6]

NIDDITCH, P. H. *An Apparatus of Variant Readings for Hume's 'Treatise of Human Nature', Including A Catalogue of Hume's Manuscript Amendments.* (55 pp.) Sheffield.

NIELSEN, H. A. 'Inference and Experience in Hume's *Enquiry*', *Phil. Papers* 5, 135–40.

NORTON, D. F. *John Home, A Sketch of the character of Mr. Hume* ... Edinburgh. (First publication; together with a republication of Home's *Diary of a Journey from Morpeth to Bath, 23 April–1 May 1776*, which first appeared in 1822) (29 pp.) [*Hume Studies* 4 (1978)]

NOXON, J. 'In Defence of "Hume's Agnosticism"', *J. Hist. Phil.* 14, 469–73. (reply to Gaskin 1976b)

NOXON, J. 'Remembering and Imagining the Past', in Livingston & King, 270–95.

NOXON, J. 'Hume's Concern With Religion', in Merrill & Shahan, 59–82.

PARENT, W. A. 'An Interpretation of Hume's *Dialogues*', *Rev. Met.* 30, 96–114.

PARENT, W. A. 'Philo's confession', *Phil. Q.* 26, 63–8.

PATTEN, S. C. 'Change, Identity and Hume', *Dialogue* 15, 664–72. (on Ashley & Stack 1974)

PATTEN, S. C. 'Hume's Bundles, Self-Consciousness and Kant', *Hume Studies* 2, 59–75.

PEARS, D. F. 'The Naturalism of Book I of Hume's *Treatise of Human Nature*', *Proc. Br. Acad.* 62, 3–22.

PENELHUM, T. 'Self-Identity and Self-Regard', in A. O. Rorty, *The Identities of Persons*, 253–80. Berkeley, etc.

PENELHUM, T. M. 'The Self in Hume's Philosophy', in Merrill & Shahan, 9–23.

POPKIN, R. H. 'Hume: Philosophical Versus Prophetic Historian', in Merrill & Shahan, 83–95.

PRICE, J. V.: see COLVER above.

PRUFER, T. 'A Reading of Hume's *A Treatise of Human Nature*', *Rev. Met.* 30, 115–19.

PUCELLE, J. 'Hume et Pascal', *Revue int. Phil.* 30, 47–63.

RATOWSKY, H. A. *The theory of ideas in the philosophy of Hume and Reid*. City U. of New York (diss.).

REINACH, A. 'Kant's Interpretation of Hume's Problem' [transl. of 1911 art. 'Kants Auffassung des Humeschen Problems', *Z. Phil. und phil. Kritik* 141, 176–209], in Merrill & Shahan, 161–88.

ROBISON, W. L. 'Hume's ontological commitments', *Phil. Q.* 26, 39–47. (sec. 2 is on Butchvarov 1959)

ROBISON, W. L. 'David Hume: Naturalist and Meta-sceptic', in Livingston & King, 23–49.

ROSE, M. C. 'The Importance of Hume in the History of Western Aesthetics', *Br. J. Aesth.* 16, 218–29.

ROTENSTREICH, N. 'Desire and Spontaneity', *Rev. Met.* 30, 39–56.

ROTWEIN, E. 'David Hume, Philosopher-Economist', in Merrill & Shahan, 117–34.

RYLEY, R. M. 'Did Warburton review Hume's *A treatise of human nature* ?', *Notes & Queries* 23, 354–5.

SAFFORD, B. C. *The concept of self in Hume's 'Treatise'.* Claremont Grad. Sch. (diss.).

SALAS ORTUETA, J. DE. 'La creencia humeana vista desde algunos autores de este siglo', *Anales del Seminario de Metafísica* 11, 135–9.

SARLOS, B. E. M. *David Hume's notion of habit and its relation to his thoughts on education.* Johns Hopkins U. (diss.).

SIEGEL, V. *David Humes Stellungnahme zur Religion unter besonderer Berücksichtigung seiner 'Natural History of Religion.'* Bonn (diss.).

SISSON, C. H. *David Hume.* (93 pp.) Edinburgh. [*PQ* 26 (1976) 365–6]

STEWART, C. 'The Moral Point of View', *Philosophy* 51, 177–87.

STOCKTON, C. N. 'Economics and the Mechanism of Historical Progress in Hume's *History*', in Livingston & King, 296–320.

STOVE, D. C. 'Hume, Induction, and the Irish', *Australas. J. Phil.* 54, 140–7. (on Adler 1975, and others) [55 (1977) 64–8]

STOVE, D. C. 'Why Should Probability Be the Guide of Life ?', in Livingston & King, 50–68.

SUTHERLAND, S. R. 'Hume on morality and the emotions', *Phil. Q.* 26, 14–23. (mainly on Kenny 1963)

THEAU, J. 'La critique de la causalité chez Malebranche et chez Hume', *Dialogue* 15, 549–64.

VENNING, C. 'Hume on Property, Commerce, and Empire in the Good Society: The Role of Historical Necessity', *J. Hist. Ideas* 37, 79–92.

VESTRE, B. *Hume and scepticism.* U. of Oslo (diss.).

WADIA, P. S. 'Miracles and common understanding', *Phil. Q.* 26, 69–81. (includes criticism of Holland 1965)

WALSH, W. H. 'The Constancy of Human Nature', in H. D. Lewis, *Contemporary British Philosophy* (Fourth Series), 274–91. London.

WARNOCK, Mary. *Imagination*, pts. 1–2. London.

WEXLER, V. G. 'David Hume's Discovery of a New Scene of Historical Thought', *Eighteenth-Century Studies* 10, 185–202.

WHITE, L. 'On a Passage by Hume incorrectly attributed to Jefferson', *J. Hist. Ideas* 37, 133–5.

YANDELL, K. E. 'Hume on Religious Belief', in Livingston & King, 109–25.

YANDELL, K. E. 'Miracles, Epistemology and Hume's Barrier', *Int. J. Phil. Relig.* 7, 391–417.

ZABEEH, F. 'Hume's Problem of Induction: An Appraisal', in Livingston & King, 69–90.

THE INDEXES

.

116

AUTHOR INDEX

Aaron, R. I.   1942, 1952, 1971
Abbagnano, N.   1948
Abbott, W. C.   1935
Acton, H. B.   1952, 1973
Adair, D.   1957
Adamson, R.   1903, 1911
Addante, P.   1971
Adler, J. E.   1975
Agnew, P. G.   1975
Ahern, D. M.   1973, 1975
Aiken, H. D. 1943, 1947, 1948 (x2)
Albee, E.   1902
Albert, F.   1914
Aldrich, V. C.   1939
Aldridge, A. O.   1949
Alejandro, J. M. de   1976
Aliotta, A.   1903
Allaire, E. B.   1963
Allan, D. M.   1927
Allard, J.-L.   1962
Allen, H. J.   1971
Allentuck, M. E.   1972
Allinson, R. E.   1976
Allison, H. E.   1972
al-Shinītī   see p. 130
Ambacher, M.   1961
Anceschi, L.   1956
Anderson, J.   1935
Anderson, R. F. 1966, 1975, 1976
Anderson, W.   1934
Andic, M.   1974
Annand, M. R.   1929, 1930
Anon.   1917, 1963
Anscombe, G. E. M.   1971, 1973
    (x2), 1974
Appeldoorn, J. G.   1903
Appleton, E.   1962
Aquila, R. E.   1974
Arce Carrascoso, J. L.   1976
Archer, R. H.   1973
Ardal, P. S.   1962, 1964, 1966,
    1972, 1976
Ardley, G.   1976
Arkin, M.   1956

Armstrong, D. M.   1960, 1961,
    1973
Armstrong, R. L.   1970
Arnoldt, E.   1907
Aronson, J.   1971
Aschenbrenner, K.   1961
Ashley, L.   1974
Aspelin, G.   1958
Atkins, J. W. H.   1951
Atkinson, R. F.   1960, 1961, 1976
Attfield, R.   1971
Augros, R.   1974
Aune, B.   1970
Ayer, A. J.   1940, 1952, 1956,
    1972, 1973
Ayers, M. R.   1968
Baczko, B.   1971
Bagolini, L.   1947, 1951, 1952,
    1976
Baier, K.   1958
Baker, K. M.   1975
Baldensperger, F.   1942
Baldinotti, C.   1974
Ballard, E. G.   1964
Bandy, W. T.   1948 (x2)
Banerjee, C.   1970
Baratono, A.   1943
Barber, K. F.   1966
Baridon, M.   1971
Barlingay, D. S.   1927
Barnes, J.   1972
Baroncelli, F.   1969, 1972, 1975
    (x2)
Barone, F.   1958
Barry, B.   1965
Bartolaso, G.   1950
Basson, A. H.   1958
Battestin, M. C.   1974
Bauch, B.   1914
Baum, R. J.   1973
Baxter, I. F. G.   1959
Bayles, M. D.   1976
Bayley, F. C.   1936
Beanblossom, R. E.   1976

LANGUAGE INDEX
(OTHER THAN ENGLISH)

1936 Ebert, Hertz, Meinecke, 1938 Wallenfels, 1939 Metz, 1943 Metz, 1951 Kastil, 1952 Brentano, 1954 Stadlin, 1955 Kruse, 1957 Heide, 1959 Stiehler, Wenzel, 1961 Lehmann-Leander, Schaefer, 1962 Krausser, Nelson, 1963 Mall, Moritz, Schaefer, 1964 & 1966 Löwisch, 1968 Gawlick, Menzel, 1969 Beck, Lauener, 1970 Risse, 1971 Hoppe, Jaeger, Mall, Stegmüller, 1973 Berger, Brandt, 1974 Brandt, Mall, Stanzel, 1975 Mall, Voigt, von Savigny, 1976 Bjelke, Hoppe, Siegel

Greek   1974 Papanoutsos

Hebrew   1954 Goldmann; see also note at end

Hungarian 1906 Gopcsa, 1967 Ludassy, 1973 Vámosi, 1976 Bence, Ludassy

Italian   1903 Aliotta, 1911 Valchera, 1913 Casazza, 1915 De Michelis, 1921 Pastore, 1923 Levi, 1924 Faggi, 1925 Mazzantini, 1926 Carlini, Libertini, 1931 Della Volpe, 1932 Zini, 1933 Dal Verme, Della Volpe, De Michelis, 1934 De Michelis, 1935 Dal Verme, Magnino, Sciacca, 1937 Bonivento, Candeloro, Dal Verme, Fabro, Giorgiantonio, Martegani, 1938 Dal Verme, Gui, 1939 Della Volpe (x2), 1941 Garin, 1942 Marchetti, 1943 Baratono, Sarno, 1947 Bagolini, 1948 Abbagnano, Bianca, Graffeo, 1949 Dal Pra (x2), Höllhuber, Paresce, 1950 Bartolaso, De Ruvo, 1951 Bagolini, Gradi, 1952 Bagolini, Bontadini, Dal Pra, Stringa, 1953 Corsi, Ricci, 1956 Anceschi, Corsi, 1957 Carlini, Chentrens & Massaron, Preti, 1958 Barone, 1959 Campanale, 1960 Castignone, 1961 Campanale, 1962 Castignone, Formigari, Giarrizzo, Molinari (x2), 1963 Molinari, Santucci, 1964 Brunetto, Castignone (x2), Molinari (x2), 1965 Grimsley & Ronco, Sabetti, Santucci (x3), 1967 Corsano, Dal Pra, Migliorini, Pennino, Ronchetti, 1968 Carabelli, Leroy, Vitiello, 1969 Baroncelli, Cappiello, Castignone, Ronchetti, Santucci, 1970 Tagliabue, 1971 Addante, Cappiello, Castignone, Giarrizzo, Lecaldano, Ronchetti, Santucci, 1972 Baroncelli, Carabelli, 1973 Dal Pra, 1974 Baldinotti (ed. Dal Pra), Restaino, Turco, Valent, 1975 Baroncelli (x2), Formigari, Lecaldano, 1976 Bagolini

Japanese   1937 Doi, 1954 Hatori, 1959 Tanaka (x2), 1963 Tanaka, 1964 Tanaka (x3), 1965 Tanaka, 1968 Tanaka, 1971 Tanaka (x2)

Norwegian 1948 Naess, 1952 Nissen, 1968 Olsen, 1971 Bjelke, Ebbing, 1973 Hiorth

Polish   1910 Bolcewicz, Sękowski, 1913 Bolcewicz, 1927 Güntzberg, 1928 Mach, 1931 Tatarkiewicz, 1948 Rutski, 1958 Hochfeldowa, Woityta, 1961 Münz, 1962 Dür, Hochfeldowa, 1963 Kozanecki, Ossowska, 1964 Obidniak, Wawrzyniak, 1966 Czarnecki, Kołakowski, 1968 Czarnecki, 1974 Jedynak

Portuguese 1967 Soveral, 1971 Enes

Romanian   1939 Florian, 1970 Neagoe, Trandafoiu, 1971 Joja, 1972 Negulescu, 1974 Gulian, 1975 Trandafoiu

Russian   1905 Vinogradov, 1925 Evthimy, 1958 Michalenko (x3), 1962 Michalenko, 1965 Meerovski, 1967 Narsky, 1975 Kostjuk

Serbo-Croat 1956 Petrović, 1959 Životić, 1964 Petrović

Spanish   1939 Romero, 1940 Vázquez, 1942 León, 1957 Matson, 1967
             Costa, 1970 Falla, Nielsen, 1972 González-Berenguer, 1973
             Salas, Rábade Romeo (x2), 1974 Mellizo, Noxon, 1975
             Rábade Romeo, Salas, 1976 Alejandro, Arce, Currás, Díaz,
             Hernández, Salas
Swedish   1914 Phalén, 1925 Hellström, 1932 Tegen, 1937 Segerstedt,
             1938 Karitz, 1941 & 1955 Hedenius, 1956 Brunius, 1958
             Aspelin, 1959 Wedberg, 1964 Jeffner

NOTE   Readers of Arabic, Chinese and Hebrew may like to know
       that three short works in these languages, not included in
       the bibliography, are recorded in the *Library of Congress
       Catalog, Books: Subjects* 1960–64, vol. 11, p. 480, and dated
       respectively 1962, 1956, and 1959. They are by Muhammad
       Fathī al-Shinīṭī, Shu-ch'un Fang, and Joseph Grunfeld.

SUBJECT INDEX